TEACHER PROFESSIONAL DEVELOPMENT CASE STUDIES

K-12, TVET, AND TERTIARY EDUCATION

JULY 2021

ASIAN DEVELOPMENT BANK

ADB

Notes:
In this publication, "$" refers to United States dollars.
ADB recognizes "Hong Kong" as Hong Kong, China; "Laos" as the Lao People's Democratic Republic; "Korea" as the
Republic of Korea; "Vietnam" as Viet Nam; and "Russia" as the Russian Federation.
All photos by ADB, unless otherwise stated.

On the cover: (1) Teachers training on information and communications technology. The Information
and Communication Technology for Innovating Rural Education Projects aim to establish a replicable model for
using ICT to bring education content, modern teaching methods, and information to poor rural schools and
communities (photo by Eric Sales/ADB). (2) A teacher instructing students during a cooling and refrigeration repair
class at the main campus of the Champasak TVET Institution (photo by ADB). (3) Students attend class in a
coeducation system at the Engineering University School and College in Dhaka (photo by Abir Abdullah/ADB).

Cover design by Kookie Trivino

Contents

Tables, Figures, and Boxes

Abbreviations

AAU	Addis Ababa University
ACE	Advancement of College Education (Republic of Korea)
ADB	Asian Development Bank
ALMA	Apoiu Lideransa liuhusi Mentoria no Aprendizajen (previously known as Professional Learning and Mentoring program) (Timor-Leste)
ATC21S	Assessment and Teaching of Twenty-First Century Skills
B.Ed.	Bachelor of Education (Ghana)
CETL	Centre of Excellence in Teaching and Learning (Bangladesh)
CoEs	Colleges of Education (Ghana)
COVID-19	coronavirus disease 2019
CTL	Center for Teaching and Learning (Republic of Korea)
DBE	Diploma in Basic Education (Ghana)
DepEd	Department of Education (Philippines)
DSP	Discipline-Specific Pedagogies Model (Singapore)
ELLN	Early Language Literacy and Numeracy
EU	European Union
FEHD	Faculty of Education and Human Development (Hong Kong, China)
FIT-ED	Foundation for Information Technology Education and Development (Philippines)
FTI	Federal Technical and Vocational Education and Training Institute (Ethiopia)
GIZ	Deutsche Gesellschaft für Internationale Zusammenarbeit
GTP	cluster and school-based teacher development group (Timor-Leste)
HEQEP	Higher Education Quality Enhancement Project (Bangladesh)
ICT	information and communication technology
IQAC	Institutional Quality Assurance Cell (Bangladesh)
ITE	Institute of Technical Education (Singapore)
K-12	Kindergarten–Grade 12
LAC	learning action cell (Philippines)
LMS	Learning Management System
M&E	monitoring and evaluation
MoES	Ministry of Education and Science of Ukraine
MoEYS	Ministry of Education, Youth and Sports (Timor-Leste)
NCTE	National Council for Tertiary Education (Ghana)
NDOE	National Department of Education (Papua New Guinea)
NGO	nongovernment organization
NTC	National Teaching Council (Ghana)
NTECF	National Teacher Education Curriculum Framework (Ghana)
NTS	National Teachers' Standards (Ghana)
PDOE	Provincial Department of Education (Papua New Guinea)

PEBL	Partnership for Enhanced and Blended Learning (Africa)
PLC	peer learning circle (Papua New Guinea)
PNG	Papua New Guinea
PPF	PNG Partnership Fund
QAA	Quality Assurance Agency (United Kingdom)
ROK	Republic of Korea
TALIS	Teaching and Learning International Survey
SBC	Standards-Based Curriculum (Papua New Guinea)
TECIP	Teacher Educators in Higher Education as Catalysts for Inclusive Practices (Ethiopia)
TEF	Teaching Excellence and Student Outcomes Framework
TEL	Technology Enhanced Learning
TEL-Hub	Technology-enhanced Learning Hub (Hong Kong, China)
TPD	teacher professional development
T-TEL	Transforming Teacher Education and Learning (Ghana)
TVET	technical and vocational education and training
UCU	University and College Union (United Kingdom)
UGC	University Grants Commission (Bangladesh)
UNESCO	United Nations Educational, Scientific and Cultural Organization
USAID	United States Agency for International Development
UK	United Kingdom
US	United States
UUK	Universities UK
VET	vocational education and training

Currency Equivalents

CURRENCY EQUIVALENTS
(as of 20 April 2021)

Currency unit – dong (D)
D1.00 = $0.000043
$1.00 = D23022.17

Currency unit – euro (€)
€1.00 = $1.21
$1.00 = €0.83

Currency unit – pound sterling (£)
£1.00 = $1.40
$1.00 = £0.71

Acknowledgments

This knowledge product was planned and developed by the Education Sector Group, Sustainable Development and Climate Change Department (SDCC) of the Asian Development Bank (ADB). It was prepared by Meekyung Shin, education specialist, SDCC; Lisa-Marie Kreibich, social sector specialist, South Asia Department; Jukka Tulivuori, social sector specialist, SDCC; and Kirsty Newman (former ADB senior education specialist), director of Programme, RISE at Oxford Policy Management, who significantly contributed to this publication.

Case studies in this knowledge product were received from the following:

For Principal from K–12: Yewon Suh, director (Office of International Cooperation, Korean Educational Development Institute, Republic of Korea).

Robin Todd, team leader (Cambridge Education, Ghana).

Ester Correia, education sector technical lead; Peter Grimes, education advisor; Antonina Marques, program manager; and Almanzo Salsinha, monitoring and evaluation officer (Partnership for Human Development Education, Timor-Leste).

Catherine Johnston, education specialist (Papua New Guinea Partnership Fund Education).

Philippine Department of Education, (Bureau for Learning Delivery, Republic of the Philippines).

Ihor Khvorostianyi, language advisor; Oksana Nesterova, project officer, and Arto Vaahtokari, chief technical advisor (Finland's Support to the Ukrainian School Reform, Finnish Consulting Group, Finland).

For technical and vocational education and training (TVET):

Yekunoamlak Alemu, PhD, assistant professor of HRD/TVET and Educational Leadership (Addis Ababa University, Ethiopia).

Maija Mäkinen, PhD, principal lecturer (JAMK University of Applied Sciences, Finland).

Iris Seet, deputy dean; William Choy, head, Pedagogic and Professional Research; and Sharon Wong, master mentor (ITE Academy, Institute of Technical Education, Singapore).

Bach Hung Truong, team leader (Supporting High-Quality TVET Institutes, GIZ Programme Reform of TVET, Viet Nam).

For higher education:

Jonathan Harle, director of programs (International Network for Advancing Science and Policy [INASP], Bangladesh and the United Kingdom).

Fiona Khandoker, programme manager (The Association of Commonwealth Universities, ACU, East Africa).

Meekyung Shin, education specialist (SDCC ADB).

Danlin Yang, assistant partnership manager; Yuen Man Tang, instructional designer; and Professor Cher Ping Lim, chair professor of Learning Technologies and Innovation (The Education University of Hong Kong, Hong Kong, China).

Technical review was provided by the following ADB Education Sector Group members: Fook Yen Chong, senior social sector specialist (Skills Development), (South East Asia Department); Zhigang Li, senior social sector specialist (South Asia Department); and Paul Vandenberg, senior economist (Economic Research and Regional Cooperation Department).

Thanks to Md. Golam Samdani Fakir, Abdullah Shams Bin Tariq, and Afroza Parvin, as well as Hank Williams who generously took time to discuss the Centres of Excellence in Teaching and Learning (CETL) initiative, share their insights and learning, provide reports and documents, and review earlier drafts of this case study. All mistakes remain the responsibility of the author.

Support in the finalization was provided by Dorothy Geronimo, senior education officer, SDCC; in close collaboration with April-Marie Gallega, Department of Communications, and Maria Theresa Mercado, editorial consultant.

This knowledge product would also not have been developed without the encouragement and overall guidance of Brajesh Panth, chief of the Education Sector Group, SDCC.

Executive Summary

Research has shown that students differ in the way they learn. How they learn relies heavily on their abilities, attitudes, and family and community backgrounds. Among the variables that influence education policies, teacher quality is recognized as the most important influence on student learning (Organisation for Economic Co-operation and Development [OECD] 2005). The teacher becomes even more crucial as students need to learn increasingly complex skills in preparation for further education and work in the 21st century. Sophisticated forms of teaching are needed to develop 21st century skills that include deep mastery of challenging content in core subjects: information, media, and technology skills; learning and innovation skills such as critical thinking, complex problem solving, effective communication and collaboration; and life and career skills, including productivity, leadership, and flexibility.

As demands for the improvement of student achievement and more complex competencies have increased, policy makers have begun to think more systematically about how to reinforce the teacher variable by attracting, developing, and retaining effective teachers (OECD 2005). These elements are all important parts of the process; a holistic approach is needed to keep a strong and qualified teaching workforce. To have an excellent group of teachers, it is necessary to attract talented people to the teaching profession through qualification management and proper remuneration. Effective education programs will also help teachers continuously develop themselves and their capabilities. Finally, the culture and incentive system must be adjusted so that excellent teachers can be recognized and can teach with pride.

Given this, governments have paid significant attention to improving the quality of teachers. This report focuses on the systemic changes needed to establish sustainable, high quality, and relevant teacher capacity development systems that ensure that improved training of teachers will continue beyond the life of a project.

This report explores relevant literature and presents case studies that showcase the provision of effective education programs in selected economies in Asia and the Pacific, and beyond, that continuously improve the teaching capabilities and expertise of teachers. It covers not only government efforts, but also the factors that enhance the effectiveness of teacher professional development programs. Unlike previous research that focused on kindergarten–grade 12 (K–12), this report includes technical and vocational education training (TVET) and higher education programs that can be adopted by developing member countries of the Asian Development Bank.

In this report, five K–12 (primary and secondary education) teacher in-service education cases from Papua New Guinea, the Philippines, Timor-Leste, Ghana, and Ukraine are discussed.

The program in Papua New Guinea partnered with the Government of Papua New Guinea to improve early years education in the country to increase the literacy and numeracy for girls and boys in elementary school. In the Philippines, the Teacher Professional Development (TPD) project aimed to formulate and test a technology-supported, blended model of TPD delivery to complement the face-to-face training-of-trainers model. In Timor-Leste—to ensure that basic education school leaders and teachers implement the new national curriculum effectively—the Government of Australia worked with the Ministry of Education and Sports in 2015 to support the design and implementation of the Professional Learning and Mentoring program (ALMA). In Ghana, a project supported by the UKAid, "Transforming Teacher Education and Learning in Ghana, (T-TEL)" envisaged a holistic package of activities focused predominantly on Ghana´s Colleges of Education. Finally, the case from Ukraine shows an example of how to improve teachers' skills in teaching Ukrainian as a second language to Ukrainian minorities. The project was supported by the Ministry for Foreign Affairs of Finland and the European Union.

Case studies from Singapore, Viet Nam, and Ethiopia explore pre-service and in-service TVET teacher training. The example from Singapore shows that increasing industry experience of TVET teachers is a key factor in obtaining up-to-date skills to design and implement demand-oriented training. The example from Viet Nam demonstrates how a Center of Excellence—in close collaboration with industry partners—ensures the continuous upgrading of teachers' competencies for the requirements of Industry 4.0 and digitalization. Continuous teacher professional development can also lead to sustainable changes in inclusive practices in TVET, as the case study from Ethiopia shows.

In higher education, the cases of universities in Bangladesh; Hong Kong, China; the Republic of Korea (ROK); the United Kingdom (UK); and Africa are introduced. In Bangladesh, 11 universities have improved their centers for teaching and learning with support from the Government of the United Kingdom. In Hong Kong, China, the universities' autonomous investments and efforts to improve online learning skills are discussed. Professional support from peers and specialists enables university teachers to explore and experiment with blended and online learning in their courses. The Government of the Republic of Korea emphasizes the importance of the education function in universities and provides the financial support to run various activities to improve teaching capacity. In the United Kingdom, the government adopts standards for professional development to guide the design, evaluation, and funding of professional learning provided to educators and evaluates universities' performance. East African universities conducted workshops to improve teacher capacity on blended learning methodology and assessment.

1 Principles of Teacher Professional Development

Introduction

The concept of teacher professional development (TPD) has gradually expanded over the years. Over the past decades, TPD has become an important global agenda that must be addressed to improve the quality of education. There is solid consensus that teachers can positively influence student learning by providing students with adequate time, constructing a proper learning atmosphere, and presenting meaningful activities (Lasley et al. 2006). Research has shown that teachers with good quality education and/or training experiences affirmatively affect their students' academic performance (Clotfelter et al. 2006; Hanushek and Rivkin 2006; Heck 2009; Ladd and Sorenson 2017; Miller and Davidson 2006; Papay and Kraft 2015; Rice 2003).

TPD can be any type of continuing education effort for teachers who are willing to improve their knowledge and skills which, in turn, improve student outcomes. There is a need to distinguish between the concepts of teacher training and TPD. Teacher training often refers to education in preparation for those who want to become teachers, whereas TPD indicates professional learning by teachers already practicing professionally. For this reason, researchers tend to favor the word "development" over "training" (Qi 2012) to emphasize the continuity of teacher education. Since these terms are often used interchangeably in teacher education and teacher learning is not a static, but ongoing process, the dichotomy is not useful from the perspective of viewing teachers as continuous learners. Therefore, rather than making a boundary between the two, discussions on teacher education tend to be enriched by defining TPD as encompassing both pre-service and in-service education.

Effective professional development is ongoing; includes training, practice, and feedback; and provides adequate time and follow-up support. Successful programs involve teachers in learning activities that are like ones they will use with their students and encourage the development of teachers' learning communities. There is growing interest in developing schools as learning organizations, and in ways for teachers to share their expertise and experience more systematically.

The concept of effective TPD for teachers is to secure and maintain a high-quality teacher workforce (Organisation for Economic Co-operation and Development [OECD] 2005). This definition, which emphasizes the effectiveness of TPD—viewing it from a more holistic point of view—stems from recognizing teaching as a profession. As professionals, teachers need TPD to continuously supplement their lack of expertise; develop competencies to respond to changes in the times, social situations, or school environment; and effectively solve various and complex problems arising in the education field. As demands for deeper and more complex student learning have intensified, practitioners, researchers, and policy makers have begun to think more systematically about how to improve teachers' learning; from recruitment, preparation, and support, to mentoring and other leadership opportunities (Darling-Hammond et al. 2017).

The idea of teachers as professionals could also be associated with the "practitioner teacher," referring to the skills, attitudes, and practices that are necessary to the profession to provide services at a certain qualitative level. Teachers' professional practice means the ability to translate professional knowledge into practice (Manasia et al. 2020). More specifically, it refers to setting goals and objectives, designing effective instructional strategies, designing evaluation and assessment tools, using feedback functions, and creating simulative learning environments that foster self-regulated learning and meet the individual needs of students.

The Importance of In-Service Teacher Professional Development

Many countries around the world stipulate through legislation and education policies the basic requirements that must be met to enter the teaching profession. United Nations Educational, Scientific and Cultural Organization's (UNESCO's) policy development guide on teachers recommends minimum requirements to go in teaching training, as well as relevant curriculum content and practicum periods leading to qualification (UNESCO 2015b). Although standards and requirements may vary from country to country, in general, the completion of a so-called "prescribed teacher training program" is a major requirement for obtaining a teaching qualification.

The programs typically consist of a blend of theoretical knowledge about teaching and a field-based practice experience (United States Agency for International Development [USAID] 2011), which are regarded as building blocks for career-long professional development. The curriculum, pedagogy, and assessment processes of pre-service programs need to be aligned with professional standards for teachers, based on specific requirements of a given country. USAID (2011) suggests elements that a successful pre-service teacher education may exhibit as follows:

   (i)   personal and professional growth as a teacher;
  (ii)   pedagogical content knowledge;
 (iii)   content knowledge;
 (iv)   classroom management;
  (v)   assessment (learners' achievement and progress through formative and summative assessment);
 (vi)   addressing special needs and challenges;
 (vii)   child development and emotional and psychological support;
(viii)   professional collaboration;
 (ix)   community engagement;
  (x)   developing a working repertoire of techniques of assessing students' learning;
 (xi)   action research; and
 (xii)   working within a system of education.

Good quality pre-service education for teachers is not enough to meet the numerous challenges that teachers face throughout their teaching life. The initial teacher education programs cannot provide them with all the competencies that are required in the actual classroom. The expectation for today's teachers is to embrace lifelong learning to be able to constantly adapt to new situations and respond to the changing demands of society in the classroom. Moreover, teachers provided with TPD opportunities commonly strengthened their job commitment and satisfaction, having positive effects over attrition and turnover (Bautista and Ortega-Ruiz 2015).

OECD has continuously stressed that initial training programs are not sufficient to cope with the changes and challenges of the globalization process, which underlines the necessity of a lifelong learning approach for the teaching profession (OECD 2005). UNESCO also highlights that to respond to the challenges in education in the 21st century, teacher education should coherently provide initial and in-service training (UNESCO/ILO/UNICEF/UNDP/EL 2018). There is global consensus that initial teacher training should be linked to continuous training.

To help students develop diverse cognitive and affective competencies required to survive in the complex future society, in-service teachers should also be given high quality and sufficient opportunities to learn and refine their own competencies. Various countries have established teacher training policies for the TPD of teachers, and accordingly, efforts have been made to develop teachers' competencies for teaching.

TPD is emphasized in education policy because the change in education can be made by various factors, but among them, the role of the teacher—who leads education in schools—is substantial. Since the development of teachers is a key issue of interest to cross-national organizations, beginning in 2008, a Teaching and Learning International Survey (TALIS)—sponsored by OECD—is now conducted every 3 years. In 2018, 48 countries from around the world participated in the survey, including 30 OECD member countries such as Finland, France, the Republic of Korea, and the United States (US), as well as non-OECD member countries such as Kazakhstan, Romania, and Viet Nam. TALIS aims to contribute to the debate about teaching as a profession. In its latest cycle in 2018, the TALIS survey selected nine main themes for inclusion. Among those, teacher instructional practices, teacher professional practices, teacher education and initial preparation, teacher feedback and development, and teacher self-efficacy are those closely related to teacher TPD.

Good TPD matters for the following reasons (Garcia and Weiss 2019):

Teachers pursue professional development opportunities to earn a master's degree, credit toward recertification or other credentials, or to gain additional qualifications to prepare for a leadership position.

(i) TPD helps teachers develop new knowledge and skills to better serve their students. This includes helping teachers update their instructional techniques in response to new research on learning and teaching processes, and to adjust to the needs of a more diverse student body.

(ii) Evidence-driven public policies have identified TPD as a key component in building systems of professional learning.

(iii) Early career support helps new teachers transition successfully from teacher training programs to being in a classroom, and continuous training helps veteran teachers adapt to changes in what they need to teach and test—and in how they need to teach and test—to accommodate changes in local and national standards.

(iv) TPD opportunities nurture a culture of learning schoolwide: (i) teachers and staff routinely develop their knowledge and skills, (ii) students see that learning is important and useful, (iii) teachers feel more respected, and (iv) teachers see ways to progress in their careers.

(v) Intense early support, continuous training, and professional development are recommended and are the norm in the most highly regarded systems where teaching is a prestigious and sought-after profession.

Because teachers are the primary agents in enacting any of the initiatives within the classroom, the provision of relevant TPD is a major engine for the improvement of both teacher competency and student academic success (Darling-Hammond et al. 2010). It has been pointed out that existing TPD programs did not account for years of teaching experience, leading some to argue that different types of programs need to be formed according to the teaching experience (Louws et al. 2017). For example, learning requirements for early career teachers could relate to concerns they experience in practice. Mid-career teachers could be supported with growth opportunities in curriculum and instruction and broader responsibilities in their job. Late-career teachers need learning opportunities about new developments such as technological innovations. By inquiring after teachers' learning needs and differentiating learning opportunities, a school leader or other facilitator of teacher learning is better able to support individual teacher learning and provide teachers with opportunities that match their needs.

Challenges of Teacher Policy in Developing Countries

According to the 2019 Global Partnership for Education report, the major challenges that many developing countries face in supporting teacher development include:

(i)   weak subject content and pedagogical knowledge, and classroom skills;
(ii) poor quality pre- and in-service teacher training and inadequate standards, certification, and accreditation procedures; and
(iii) a lack of ongoing support from head teachers, schools, and districts.

The importance of TPD is emphasized in teacher policy because the role of the teacher has the most direct and immediate influence on changes in education. The importance of teachers in education is in line with the very need for TPD to increase the professionalism of teachers. In other words, it is necessary to acquire new knowledge, skills, attitude—and even wisdom—according to social changes and changes in teaching and learning methods through TPD programs, and to increase the professionalism of teachers through continuous efforts. By failing to provide teachers with broad access to effective TPD, teachers' effectiveness, sense of purpose, and career advancement opportunities will stagnate (Garcia and Weiss 2019).

The UNESCO (2015a) monitoring report indicates that many developing countries have tried to strengthen policy frameworks and innovative programs to boost the status of the teaching profession. Among those efforts, securing the necessary number of teachers and providing suitable TPD for their development is considered a priority.

The lack of teachers is also a critical issue that must be addressed in the discussion of teacher quality. In many developing countries, the problem of teacher shortages has emerged as a significant education policy concern. According to estimations by the UNESCO Institute of Statistics (2016), countries must recruit 68.8 million teachers by 2030, including 24.4 million primary school teachers, and 44.4 million secondary school teachers. The South Asia region—which has the second-largest teacher shortage—must recruit 15 million teachers by 2030; 4.1 million at the primary level and 10.9 million at the secondary. Because of the insufficient number of teachers and the frequent teacher turnover in this region, the average student-teacher ratio stands at 34:1 in primary schools and 29:1 in secondary schools.

The problem of recruiting teachers in developing countries includes not only the absolute scale of securing teachers necessary for expanding education opportunities, but also the qualitative aspect of retaining qualified teachers. In most Asian countries, candidates for teacher training must hold a minimum of a 12-year or equivalent school certificate regardless of the level at which they want to teach. In many countries—such as Mongolia, Pakistan, and Uzbekistan—candidates are required to have a 4-year degree program (UNESCO Bangkok Office 2015). In Viet Nam, student teachers follow a 3-year program of college education to teach at the primary and lower secondary level, while those wishing to teach at the upper secondary level must undertake a 4-year higher education program (Nguyen 2003). In 2017, Cambodia—which makes a lot of effort to promote the innovative development of teacher education—introduced a new regulation that all pre-service teachers need to hold a bachelor's degree to be able to teach regardless of school level, according to the Teacher Policy Action Plan (Ministry of Education, Youth and Sport [MoEYS] 2015).

Although selective qualifications are required to enter the teaching profession, there may be cases where such requirements are adjusted to solve the problem of teacher shortages for some countries (Mulkeen et al. 2017). In these cases, policy makers might be challenged in securing the required number of teachers and may allow teachers to teach without having had prior training in the area (Villegas-Reimers 2003). Therefore, continuing TPD is even more important in countries where teachers do not have all the academic preparation they should have.

Teacher salary is another big challenge to be addressed in education policies in developing countries. Improving teachers' salaries constitutes strong leverage in countries willing to enhance the status and the attractiveness of the teaching profession. Low and inadequate salaries can act as a disincentive for qualified candidates to join and remain in the profession (UNESCO 2015a). Attracting excellent human resources and establishing a reward system becomes an important policy priority. For instance, Ethiopia reported that the salaries of teachers at the primary and secondary levels are two tiers above those of other government employees. In Armenia, legal provisions ensure that salaries for the teaching profession may not be lower than the average salary of some other national institutions (UNESCO 2015a). In Uzbekistan, teachers' salaries increased fivefold between 2005 and 2009. In Mongolia, salaries increased by 15% in 2014 (UNESCO Bangkok Office 2015).

Teachers' salaries remain low in some countries in comparison to those of other professions. In Sri Lanka, teachers seem to earn up to one-third less than the average income. Cambodia is also one of the representative countries known for having a lower salary for teachers compared to other professions (UNESCO Bangkok Office 2015). The average teachers' salary in the Philippines is less than one-sixth of the average in the Association of Southeast Asian Nation countries (*The Philippine Star* 2019). In some developing countries, low teacher salaries could be a factor contributing to teachers engaging in other side jobs, leaving teaching, and even having increasing debts. Consequently, many developing countries agree that teachers' salaries should be increased, particularly to attract and retain better candidates to the profession. Appropriate salary level is still being debated in establishing teacher policy.

Shifting Teacher Professional Development: A Competence-Based Model

TPD can be a powerful tool for those who aspire to develop the knowledge and skills needed to reach higher student outcomes. Guskey (2000) defines TPD as "those processes and activities designed to enhance the professional knowledge, skills, and attitudes of educators so that they might, in turn, improve the learning of students." Since the success and dynamism of the education system—as well as achievement of education goals—require an increase in the level of knowledge and ability of teachers on a very practical level, the strengthening and development of the "teacher sector" would be the heart and soul of education (Moghtadaie and Taji 2018).

Early TPD often focused on providing teachers with up-to-date subject knowledge based on a certain belief that continuous learning and review of both content and instruction is an essential component of the teaching profession (Barber and Mourshe 2007). Accordingly, professional development programs for teachers have revolved around knowledge bases for teachers, which include content knowledge, pedagogical content knowledge, and procedural knowledge (Luneta 2012). From this perspective, effective teaching depends on how a teacher selects and integrates various strands from those three knowledge bases to create valuable learning opportunities. In other words, effective teaching is "the presentation of content to learners" using a suitable form of instruction (Guskey 2003; Luneta 2011; Murray 2010). Effective TPD should encourage teachers to sharpen and deepen their knowledge and skills necessary to provide effective instruction and assess student progress.

Teachers' knowledge bases are still the undeniable fundamental elements of TPD. However, such TPD approach has been shaped more sophisticatedly by adopting the concept of "competence" through highlighting the multiple layers and complexity of teachers' actual teaching practice and context. In recent literature, "teacher competence" is considered a key mechanism of TPD in creating a quality teaching force where teachers' work has become much more complex and demanding to meet the challenges of the future (Ananiadou and Claro 2009; Blömeke 2017; European Commission 2013 and 2019; Metsapelto et al. 2020; Moghtadaie and Taji 2018; Southeast Asia Teachers Competency Framework [SEA-TCF] 2018; Sumaryanta et al. 2018; Zhao 2010).

Defined holistically, competence is regarded as "the possession and development of a complex combination of integrated skills, knowledge, attitudes and values displayed in the context of task performance" (Education International 2011, p. 21). It is, therefore, differentiated from "skill," which is defined as the ability to use one's knowledge effectively and readily in execution or performance (Merriam-Webster Open Dictionary). The European Commission (2013) has emphasized that teachers today need competencies—such as having critical, evidence-based attitudes enabling them to respond to students' outcomes; new evidence from inside and outside the classroom; and professional dialogue—that will enable them to constantly innovate and adapt. The concept of competence in teaching thus encompasses the following features (European Commission 2013, p. 10):

(i)   it involves tacit and explicit knowledge, cognitive and practical skills, as well as dispositions (motivation, beliefs, value orientations, and emotions);
(ii) it enables teachers to meet complex demands, by mobilizing psychosocial resources in context, coherently deploying them;
(iii) it empowers the teacher to act professionally and appropriately in a situation;
(iv) it helps ensure teachers' undertaking of tasks effectively (achieving the desired outcome) and efficiently (optimizing resources and efforts); and
(v)   it can be demonstrated to a certain level of achievement along a continuum.

Consequently, TPD that was designed and based on teachers' competencies would have powerful effects on student learning and achievement. TPD that was conducted without considering various aspects of teaching from a competence perspective has shown to cause problems such as poor self-knowledge, lack of knowledge of students in a multicultural context, low managerial skills and poor pedagogical competence, deficiency of reflection, and the ability to be self-critical (Nguyen 2003).

In Asia, teaching competence standards has been developed for 11 countries of the Southeast Asian Ministers of Education Organization (SEAMEO) that would serve as a guide in identifying the instructional design of capacity-building strategies for teacher training programs. SEAMEO INNOTECH identifies the common domains of teaching standards for Southeast Asia in Figure 1.

The meaning of each domain is as follows:

(i)   Professional knowledge: The mastery of content and methodology for teaching.
(ii) Professional skills: Pedagogies, classroom management, and learner assessment.
(iii) Professional characteristics: Personal traits (e.g., being responsible, punctual, etc.).
(iv) Professional and personal ethical standards and values: Moral, good role model, etc.
(v)   Professional development and lifelong learning: Participation in professional teacher organizations and activities, demonstrates a desire to enhance the teaching profession, etc.

After several years, the SEAMEO INNOTECH model takes on a more practical and developmental look as in Figure 2.

Figure 1:   Major Strands of Teaching Competence in Southeast Asia

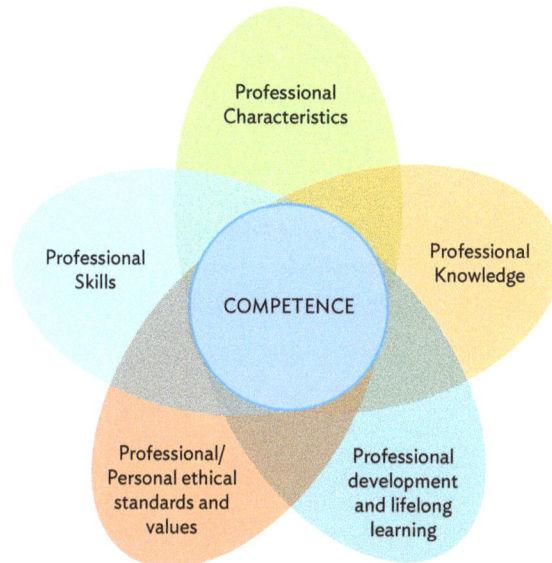

Professional
Characteristics

Professional
Skills

COMPETENCE

Professional
Knowledge

Professional/
Personal ethical
standards and
values

Professional
development
and lifelong
learning

Source: Southeast Asian Ministers of Education Organization-INNOTECH. 2010. p. 76.

Figure 2:   Southeast Asia Teachers Competency Framework

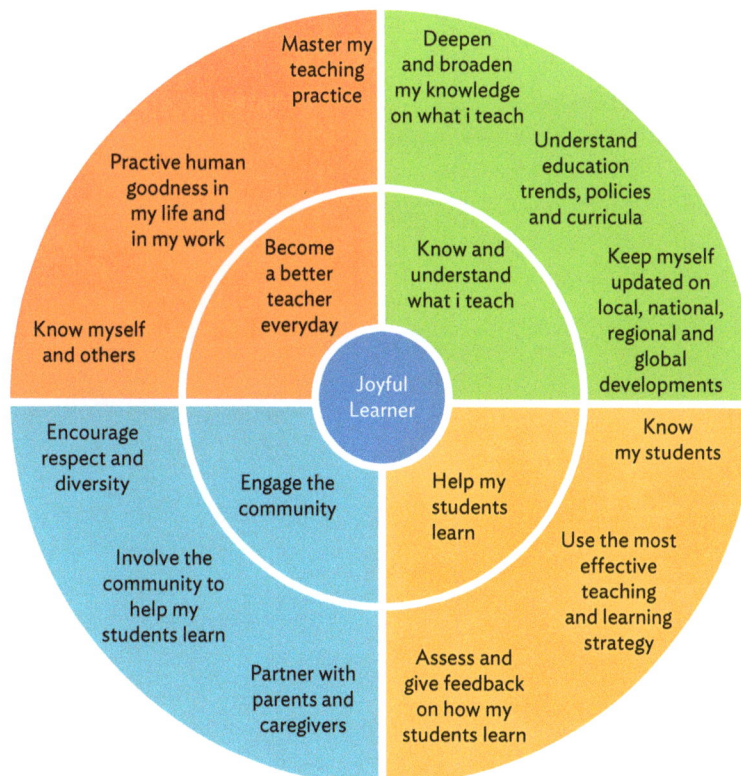

Master my
teaching
practice

Deepen
and broaden
my knowledge
on what i teach

Practive human
goodness in
my life and
in my work

Understand
education
trends, policies
and curricula

Become
a better
teacher
everyday

Know and
understand
what i teach

Keep myself
updated on
local, national,
regional and
global
developments

Know myself
and others

Joyful
Learner

Encourage
respect and
diversity

Know
my students

Engage the
community

Help my
students
learn

Involve the
community to
help my
students learn

Use the most
effective
teaching
and learning
strategy

Partner with
parents and
caregivers

Assess and
give feedback
on how my
students learn

Source: Southeast Asia Teachers Competency Framework (SEA-TCF). 2018. p. 7.

The SEA-TCF model takes a major step forward from the previous model by clearly presenting four essential competencies that teachers in Southeast Asia should possess for optimal performance. These are:

(i) **Knowing and understanding what to teach** is the ability of teachers to deepen and broaden their knowledge on what to teach, understand education trends, policies, and curricula, and be updated on local, national, regional, and global developments;

(ii) **Helping students learn** is the ability to know their students, use the most effective teaching and learning strategy, and assess and give feedback on how students learn;

(iii) **Engaging the community** is the ability to partner with parents and caregivers, involve the community to help students learn, and encourage respect and diversity;

(iv) **Becoming a better teacher every day** is the ability to know oneself and others, practice human goodness and then master the teaching practice (SEA-TCF 2018, p. 5).

Furthermore, these four competencies consist of 12 general competencies, 31 enabling competencies, and 136 success descriptors in detail. This complex model attempts to be a helpful guide in improving the performance of teachers across Southeast Asia, underlining that competencies should be interpreted based on local context and specific needs.

In the more recent competency-based teacher education movement outside of Asia, 21st century competencies are seen as necessary to navigate contemporary and future life, shaped by technology that is changing workplaces and lifestyles (Caena and Redecke 2019). They underline new skills, but also emphasize existing ones, thus equipping individuals for new ways of thinking, ways of working, and tools for working and living in the world, as outlined in the Assessment and Teaching of Twenty-First Century Skills (ATC21S) framework (Binkley et al. 2012). ATC21S is an international project consortium that incorporates academic institutions, policy makers, technology businesses (Cisco, Intel, Microsoft) and coordinated by the University of Melbourne which aimed to promote education assessment reform for direct impact on teaching and learning 21st-century skills (Griffin et al. 2012).

In the ATC21S framework, ways of thinking include creativity and innovation, critical thinking, problem-solving, learning-to-learn, and metacognition. The sub-elements of each competence within the framework of the ATC21S are as follows: (i) ways of working including communication, collaboration, and teamwork; (ii) tools for working containing information; and (iii) information and communication technology (ICT) literacy (Griffin et al. 2012). Living in today's world magnifies the significance of local and global citizenship, life and career development, and personal and social responsibility.

The framework defines competence as the ability to adjust the skill performance to the demands of the situation. This view encompasses the quality and transferability of skills over time and context, acknowledging the fact that no one performs a skill at the same level or operates at their maximum every time (Griffin and Care 2014). It is necessary to pay attention to the model presented in Figure 3 by OECD (Guerriero, ed. 2017) so that teachers have the competence to respond to the more complex and diverse needs of the 21st century.

This conceptual framework of teachers' professional competence encompasses the professional knowledge base of teachers—content and pedagogical knowledge—as well as affective motivational competencies. Teaching also requires decision-making skills and professional judgment that allow teachers to analyze and evaluate specific contexts or learning episodes and—drawing on their knowledge and competencies—to make decisions about teaching approaches and instruction. Teaching approaches refer to curriculum and lesson planning, selecting and applying sets of teaching methods, classroom management, student assessment, and so on while instruction is the implementation of these approaches in the classroom (Guerriero, ed. 2017).

Figure 3:   Conceptual Framework of Teachers' Professional Competence

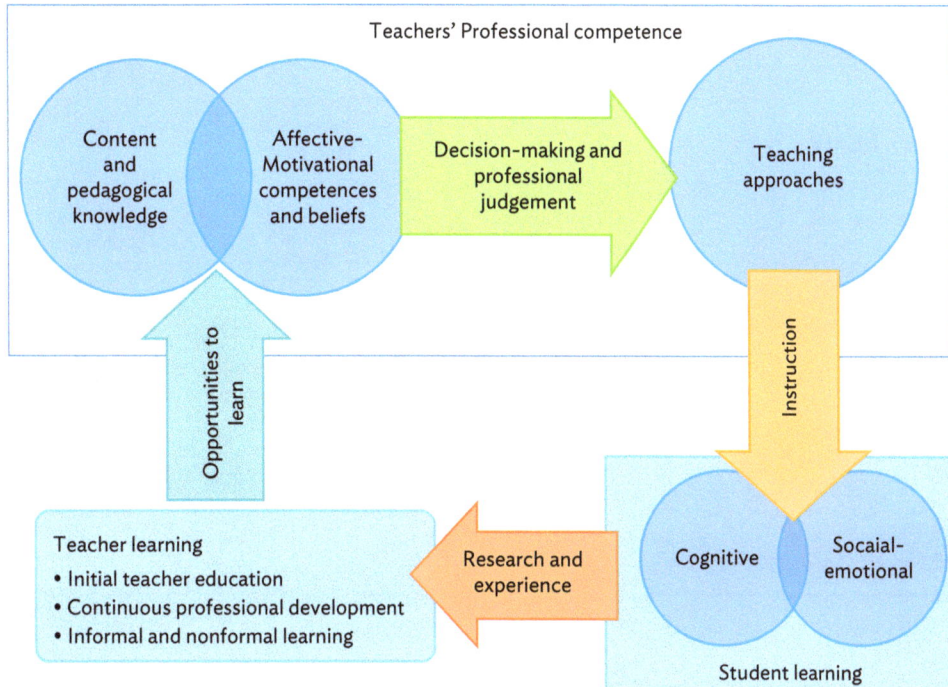

Teachers' Professional competence

Content and pedagogical knowledge

Affective-Motivational competences and beliefs

Decision-making and professional judgement

Teaching approaches

Instruction

Opportunities to learn

Teacher learning
• Initial teacher education
• Continuous professional development
• Informal and nonformal learning

Research and experience

Cognitive

Socaial-emotional

Student learning

Source: S. Guerriero, ed. 2017. *Pedagogical knowledge and the changing nature of the teaching profession.* Paris: OECD Publishing. http://dx.doi.org/10.1787/9789264270695-en. p. 261.

At present, "a multidimensional adapted process model of teaching" (MAP) proposed by Metsapelto and colleagues in 2020 seems to be the most up-to-date teacher competence model. The MAP (Metsapelto et al. 2020) aims to conceptualize in detail what teacher education should strive to foster in the preparation of future teachers and to determine the key competency domains that TPD needs to focus on, based on an intensive literature review on teacher research. Even though the MAP is originally derived from the Blömeke et al. (2015) model of teacher competencies, it is taking a much more advanced aspect by adding various detailed concepts and principles of operation.

As shown in Figure 4, dimensions of competencies are divided into five domains. Among those, the cognitive competencies include the "knowledge base for teaching and learning" and "cognitive skills." The remaining three domains belong to noncognitive competencies, according to Metsapelto et al. (2020). They explain each domain as (i) "social skills" focusing on how a teacher manages relations with others, (ii) "personal orientations" involving the management of oneself in the role of teacher, and (iii) "professional well-being" concentrating on how a teacher manages their work. In addition to dimensions of teachers' competencies, the MAP model places great emphasis on situation-specific cognitive processes affecting the navigation of moment-to-moment situations in the specific time, place, and social context of the classroom and school. Furthermore, it specifies teachers' professional practices at three levels, including concrete classroom practices with the individual and group level, practices and collaboration at school community with the organization level, and activities at the local, national, and global level. Finally, it introduces the term "teacher effectiveness" to illustrate the contribution of teaching to student outcomes.

Figure 4:   **Multidimensional Adapted Process Model of Teaching**

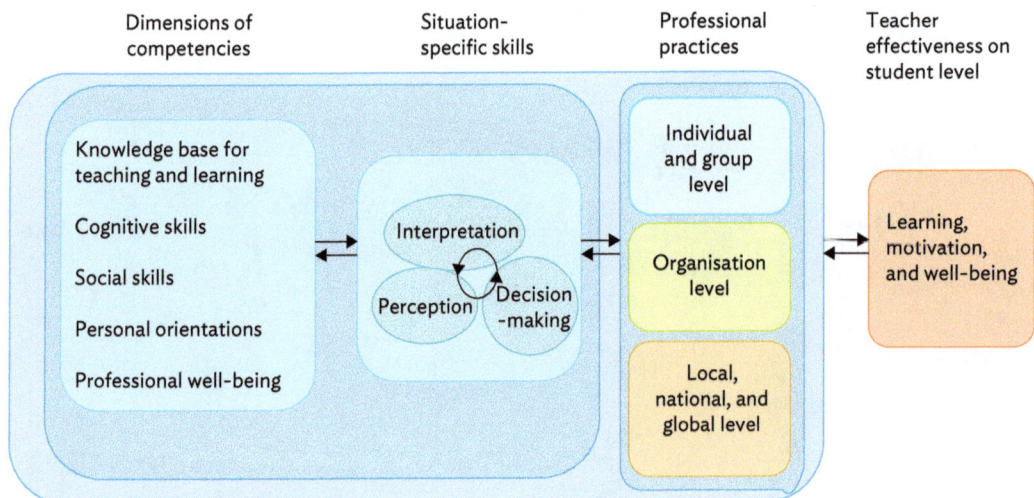

Source: R. L. Metsapelto et al. 2020. *Conceptual framework of teaching quality: A multidimensional adapted process model of teaching.* OVET Project Working Paper. p. 6.

We use the term "process model" to convey the view that teachers' skills, knowledge, and behaviors instigate meaningful learning and growth at the student level. Students, however, are not seen as recipients of information flowing unidirectionally from teachers, but as active agents who influence the learning process and whose characteristics, initiatives, and active efforts evoke a range of instructional patterns and responses among teachers. This is indicated by a two-way arrow between the teacher and student components of the model (Metsapelto et al. 2020, pp. 5–6). The MAP model presumes bilateral linkage between various components in the model, demonstrating the complexity of dynamic interaction among underlying competencies, situation-specific skills, and practices manifested in action.

So far, various teacher-competence models have been explored. These various efforts to conceptualize teachers' competencies and the mechanism of subcomponents are expected to present a clear vision for designing successful TPD.

New Dimension of Teacher Professional Development

Recent discussions are focused on how to design learning experiences of TPD, which has an impact on teachers' knowledge and practices. In this regard, seven characteristics of effective TPD proposed by Darling-Hammond and colleagues (2017) provide useful insights for planning and constructing new TPD models. Effective TPD

   (i)   is content-focused;
   (ii) incorporates active learning, utilizing adult learning theory;
   (iii) supports collaboration, typically in job-embedded contexts;
   (iv) uses models and modeling of effective practice;
   (v)   provides coaching and expert support;
   (vi) offers opportunities for feedback and reflection; and
   (vii) is of sustained duration.

Such an effective TPD model would be of great help to teachers who are eager to evaluate and update their competencies while in the teaching profession as it is a crucial responsibility of teachers to construct environments and opportunities for in-depth learning experiences that encourage students to discover and improve their new abilities. Teachers are called on to be activators of meaningful learning and have the task of recognizing, connecting, and adapting students' talents to suit the situation by showing creativity in a variety of learning contexts. Teachers need to span several roles: they are "mentors who build relationships of trust with students; orchestrators of individual and group learning; alchemists who compound strategies, techniques, and resources to spark students' creativity; welders who connect bits and pieces of knowledge and activities into a meaningful whole; and team players, understanding and deploying their own and others' potential to the full" (Caena 2017).

There are nine proposed areas of teachers' competence as valuable components of TPD beyond the preconceived ideas (Selvi 2010):

(i) **Field competencies**: This is related to the subject content knowledge. In the 21st century, it is not about sharing the information from the textbook, it is about facilitating the students to interact with the content through effective questioning.

(ii) **Research competencies**: To develop self and others, researching the subject, latest developments in education, change in the pedagogical approaches, use of technology in lessons help teachers to develop themselves, and become effective and efficient teachers.

(iii) **Curriculum competencies**: The role of the teacher in the development of curriculum and implementation is very important.

(iv) **Emotional competencies**: This is the ability to deal positively with the emotional needs of the students. It complements a positive learning environment and, hence, learning.

(v) **Lifelong learning competencies**: One of the most important competencies to develop oneself and be a lifelong learner and become a role model to the students, which will inspire them to be lifelong learners.

(vi) **Sociocultural competencies**: Deals with the awareness of sociocultural environments of learners and teachers, democracy and human rights issues, local and national values, and team and collaborative work with others. A teacher's sociocultural competencies advocate a humanistic approach and practice of social theories.

(vii) **Communication competencies**: To achieve the goal—the learning in lessons—effective inter- and intrapersonal communication skills are vital.

(viii) **ICT competencies**: Integration of ICT in lessons is one of the non-negotiables in an effective lesson.

(ix) **Environmental competencies**: Involves knowledge and skills regarding the environment, management of ecological resources, feasible uses of natural resources, and keeping a clean environment. These are required to deal with ecological and environmental safety.

Future-oriented teaching competencies are often emphasized in certain areas such as digital competence. Society is putting pressure on schools to prepare students for the deepening digital era and have the necessary competencies, but teachers still do not seem to be ready to practice such competencies. Teachers should be able to integrate digital technologies in education and should help students use the internet responsibly, critically, and creatively to complement their social interactions and life opportunities. There is a consensus that digital competencies are key for all citizens to engage in lifelong learning, and to facilitate personal fulfillment and development, employability, social inclusion, and active citizenship (European Council 2018).

The world is experiencing a radical transition from the traditional face-to-face teaching and learning method to distance learning, spurred by the coronavirus disease 2019 (COVID-19) pandemic. With an unprecedented expansion of online learning methods, teachers need to learn new online tools and prepare class content suitable for the distance learning method. Digital competence refers to the ability to understand and express information that is essential in the digital age and is required not only for students, but also for teachers. However, it tends to be viewed as a skill that is only needed by students in general. With the changes brought on by COVID-19, additional changes in perception toward teachers' essential competencies to prepare for a future education are expected to occur and this change will urge creative attempts to develop not only the content, but also the methods of teacher education through TPD.

As the education field has become increasingly more unpredictable and dynamic, the paradigm is shifting away from the traditional view of the teacher's professionalism as a conveyer of subject knowledge. In other words, the important competencies that teachers must have include the following: (i) reorganization and autonomous management of the curriculum; (ii) the creation, maintenance, and growth of the school community; and (iii) understanding and promotion of the students' holistic growth process. Therefore, it is also crucial for TPD to provide an opportunity for teachers to grow themselves by participating in learning through autonomy and not passively by others.

In this respect, a "teacher learning community" can be a good alternative to TPD to enhance teacher professionalism. The teacher learning community is a group of teachers who learn, explore, and practice collaboratively to elevate teacher professionalism and promote student learning. It shares values and norms, focuses on the learning of teachers and students, and is characterized by cooperation among community members. An innovative TPD environment needs to be constructed in which all participants can expose aspects of themselves and explore their subjectivities (Crecci and Fiorentini 2018). In these environments, the emergence of a different vision is possible.

Teacher Professional Development in Technical and Vocational Education and Training and Higher Education

Successful TPD models usually consist of most—or all—of the seven characteristics of effective TPD as explained earlier by Darling-Hammond and colleagues (2017). A TPD model, which is a complex mixture of those important characteristics, is suitable for addressing the diverse needs of learners (participants in TPD) in differing settings, across grades and subject areas of K–12, TVET training, and even higher education. Since the growing demand for TVET has increased the demand for TVET teachers in many developing countries where teachers often do not possess the competencies needed to teach effectively (Njenga 2019), a relevant TPD model can lead to the empowerment of TVET teachers lacking adequate skills, experience, and exposure to current industry practices and modern technology.

This is the same for the teaching of higher education. The teaching capacity of university professors in developing countries leaves much room for improvement. For example, as of 2019, less than 5% of all university faculty and staff in Lao People's Democratic Republic have a doctorate (Hayden 2019). In developing countries, it is difficult to expect high quality tertiary education due to various factors such as limited government investment, lack of capacity, and various infrastructure and staffing problems. However, insufficient teaching competence hinders the development of higher education. Academic staff members are the most important resource for higher education and providing practicable TPD opportunities for them is enormously important in developing their solid content knowledge, effective teaching and communication skills, and some level of research competence (ADB 2011).

Implications for Policy Makers

Examples of successful TPD in raising student achievement can help policy makers and practitioners better understand what quality teacher professional learning looks like. Examples of how policy can help support and incentivize the kind of evidence-based TPD are as follows (Darling-Hammond et al. 2017):

(i)   Policy makers could adopt standards for professional development to guide the design, evaluation, and funding of professional learning provided to educators. These standards might reflect the features of effective professional learning as well as standards for implementation.

(ii) Policy makers and administrators could evaluate and redesign the use of time and school schedules to increase opportunities for professional learning and collaboration, including participation in professional learning communities, peer coaching and observations across classrooms, and collaborative planning.

(iii) States, districts, and schools could regularly conduct needs assessments using data from staff surveys to identify areas of professional learning most needed and desired by educators. Data from these sources can help ensure that professional learning is not disconnected from practice and supports the areas of knowledge and skills educators want to develop.

(iv) State and district administrators could identify and develop expert teachers as mentors and coaches to support learning in their area(s) of expertise for other educators.

(v)   States and districts can provide technology-facilitated opportunities for professional learning and coaching, using available funding to address the needs of rural communities and provide opportunities within the district and/or school for collaboration.

(vi) Policy makers can provide flexible funding and continuing education components for learning opportunities that include sustained engagement in collaboration, mentoring, and coaching, as well as institutes, workshops, and seminars.

Papua New Guinea—Enhancing Teaching Skills through the Papua New Guinea–Australia Partnership

Author: Catherine Johnston, Education Specialist, Papua New Guinea Partnership Fund Education

Papua New Guinea Partnership Fund (2019). Elementary student writing in Madang Province, Papua New Guinea

Papua New Guinea Partnership Fund (2017–April 2020)

The Papua New Guinea (PNG) Partnership Fund (PPF) was established in 2017 as part of the PNG-Australia Partnership to expand the coverage of evidence-based education interventions. The program partners with the Government of PNG to improve the early years of education in the country, with a focus on inclusive teaching and learning practices that increase literacy and numeracy for girls and boys in elementary school.

Context

PNG comprises the eastern half of New Guinea island and more than 600 nearby islands and is the largest country in the Pacific region. PNG is one of the world's most ethnically diverse countries, with more than 850 indigenous languages spoken. The World Bank classifies PNG as a lower-middle-income country (World Bank 2020). It is estimated that 85% of the population—or 7.3 million people—live in rural remote areas spread across difficult terrain, often isolated due to poor or nonexistent transport links and communications (National Department of Education [NDOE] 2016). Over a quarter (2.4 million out of 8.1 million people) of the population live in extreme poverty. The rural population is predominately engaged in subsistence and cash income agricultural activities. PNG is still one of some 30 countries worldwide considered to be off-track in achieving Sustainable Development Goal 1: No poverty (World Data Lab 2019).

PNG Education System, Enrollment Rates, and Standards

PNG's national education system is highly decentralized, but lacks both finance and capacity at the national, provincial, and district levels, which has seriously hindered the achievement of education outcomes across the whole system.

The PNG education system is in a period of transition from a previous 3-6-4 structure (Elementary Preparatory to Grade 2; Primary 3 to Grade 8; and Secondary 9 to Grade 12) to a 1-6-6 structure that will see a preparatory year of early childhood followed by 6 years each for primary and secondary. This transition presents significant challenges for the early grades of primary education. The elementary schools have primarily been the responsibility of district level education authorities with little oversight from the provincial level and the NDOE has relied heavily on an underqualified volunteer teacher workforce.

PNG's national education system is highly decentralized, but a lack of both hard and soft capacities at the national, provincial, and district levels, has seriously hindered the achievement of education outcomes across the whole system. Lack of coordination between the national and subnational levels—together with limited planning, budgeting, and monitoring of expenditure and outcomes—seriously undermines the provision of quality education (Kukari 2018).

Despite a high national gross enrollment rate for basic education of 96% as of 2014, significant national disparities persist (NDOE 2016). Enrollment rates in elementary schools reached 80% in 2014, but at all levels of education, there are high rates of absenteeism and repetition, low retention and transition, and—based on the National Education Plan Addendum—many overaged children (ADB 2012). The government's Tuition Free Fee (TFF) policy has likely contributed to the bubble evident in enrollment figures over the past 7 years. As of 2016, only 57% of Grade 8 female students and 61% of Grade 8 male students transitioned to secondary education (NDOE 2016). The Gender Parity Index deteriorates as females move through the system. With the end of the government's TFF scheme—having moved to a subsidy scheme involving parental contribution to school fees—enrollment and retention disparities are likely to remain.

Learning outcomes are poor at all school levels. Early grade reading assessments conducted from 2011 to 2013 found that children's critical pre-reading skills were 2 years behind the curriculum target and that students took 5 years to attain some reading skill objectives required by the first-grade curriculum (Macdonald and Vul 2018). The 2018 Pacific Islands Literacy Numeracy Assessment (PILNA) found that only 38% of PNG Grade 3 students achieved at or above the minimum expected proficiency level (Figure 5 in ACER 2019) . Students in urban schools outperformed those in nonurban schools and provincial literacy and numeracy results varied significantly (Global Partnership for Education [GPE] 2018).

Figure 5:   2018 Pacific Islands Literacy Numeracy Assessment Report for Papua New Guinea

PNG PILNA 2018

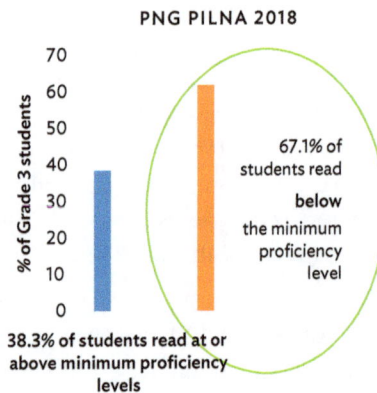

67.1% of students read **below** the minimum proficiency level

38.3% of students read at or above minimum proficiency levels

Source: Australian Council for Educational Research (ACER). 2019. *Papua New Guinea Pacific Islands Literacy and Numeracy Assessment (PILNA) 2018 Results.* Suva.

To improve education standards, the NDOE introduced the Standards-Based Curriculum (SBC) in 2015 to replace the previous Outcome-Based Education curriculum. The SBC sets standards for teacher training and professional development, student assessment, school inspections, and school governance. However, insufficient curriculum materials, a dire lack of quality age-appropriate reading materials to support children's early grade literacy learning, and poor-quality school infrastructure—including teacher housing and classrooms—remain significant barriers to quality education provision (Smith and Simoncini 2018). Most elementary teachers have not received all required curriculum resources and often have little more than the teacher's guide to work from. Some socialization of the curriculum has been offered, but most have not received any SBC training.

Reviews have consistently identified the deteriorating quality and quantity of PNG's teacher education and professional development system. The proportion of trained teachers at all education levels remains low due to limited access to formal education, low matriculation rates, and a rapidly expanding education system that has led to significant teacher shortfalls, particularly with the introduction of elementary. This has resulted in the mass recruitment of underqualified teachers. Only 50% of elementary teachers are qualified (Education Management Information System [EMIS] 2016) and community volunteer teachers are often used to fill teacher shortages. These volunteer teachers are not paid by the NDOE and, therefore, rely on community contributions or livelihood activities for their income. This has contributed to low teacher motivation and high teacher absenteeism in elementary schools. An analysis of education policy and practice by the Pacific Benchmarking for Education Results (2016) found—among others—significant challenges impacting teacher quality, including (i) inconsistent and insufficient professional development of teachers at the national and subnational levels; (ii) variations in teacher evaluation, pedagogical guidance, and support, partly due to limited training of head teachers; (iii) considerable disparity in the skills and competencies of teachers to effectively carry out classroom assessments, limiting the use of assessments to inform interventions to improve student learning; (iv) the lack of adequate access to curriculum materials in schools; and (v) variable implementation of the curriculum due to teachers' variable competency and capacity (Education Quality Assessment Program [EQAP] 2016).

In-service teacher training in PNG is fragmented and previous attempts to establish a continuous teacher professional development (TPD) system that prioritizes feedback and support post training has not been sustained beyond initial pilots. Provincial education departments provide 5 to 10 days of in-service teacher training each year, but its implementation is not consistent or systematic. If training is offered, it focuses on orientation rather than skill building on specific teaching strategies. Peer learning opportunities—such as teacher networks, teacher learning circles, and school-based teacher professional development—are limited. Coaches and mentors to provide school-based support and guidance to improve quality practice in the classroom are lacking, as is the quality assurance on TPD provision throughout the country.

Table 1:   Papua New Guinea Partnership Fund Education Grantees
Target Provinces, Districts, and Focus Area

Rapidly Improving Education Standards	Together for Education	Pikinini Kisim Save
Partnerships		
Save the Children, Callan Services, Summer Institute of Linguistics	World Vision, Child Fund, Library for All, CIMC, and University of Canberra	CARE International, Adventist Development and Relief Agency (ADRA), University of Goroka, and the Queensland University of Technology
Target provinces		
Autonomous Region of Bougainville, Eastern Highlands Province, and East Sepik Province	Central, Madang, and Morobe Provinces	Jiwaka, Simbu, Western Highlands, and West New Britain
Project Focus		
Rapidly Improving Education Standards (RISE) focuses on intensive teacher training and community literacy actions to increase the frequency of literacy and numeracy activities that elementary children are exposed to each day at home and in the community. RISE also invests in early childhood education to ensure children are school-ready when they start elementary.	Together for Education (T4E) emphasizes school governance and parental engagement to drive quality improvements at the school level. Alongside teacher training and quality reading resources, T4E is strengthening how elementary schools develop and execute their School Learning Improvement Plans.	Pikinini Kisim Save (PKS) focuses on improving the qualifications of elementary teachers and the quality of provincial and district officers to support elementary school improvement. CARE International will utilize its community leadership project model to drive change in the community's commitment toward education.

Source: Papua New Guinea Partnership Fund (2019) Baseline synthesis report.

Intervention

In March 2017, the PNG Partnership Fund (PPF) was established through the PNG-Australia Partnership. Three education consortia have been working with the NDOE and respective provincial authorities as part of this program to improve early grade literacy and numeracy outcomes for elementary students since 2018 (Table 1).

All projects focus on enhancing the quality of instruction, effective utilization of the SBC, and increasing the quantity and quality of teaching and learning resources for elementary teachers and children. Each project has prioritized support to inclusion, with a focus on gender and disability in all outcome areas.

With TPD, each consortium provides at least 10 days of in-service teacher training annually. Typically, this has included up to 5 days focused on foundational literacy teaching to support SBC English, up to 5 days focused on foundational numeracy teaching to support SBC Mathematics, and up to 5 days for a range of supplementary topics, including gender and disability inclusion, child protection, and positive discipline. The in-service training was provided during the three school term breaks of the year and repeated on an annual basis for a different cohort of elementary teachers. Each consortium engaged provincial and/or district education authorities in supporting the delivery of in-service training, a key approach to capacity development of subnational education authorities and sustainability. Due to the lack of teaching and learning resources in elementary schools, teachers were provided with high quality readers and storybooks to promote reading and teaching resources to support SBC delivery.

To further complement the training and ensure teachers were supported to apply strategies they had learned during training, each nongovernment organization (NGO) consortia developed a specific strategy for post-training TPD. These strategies were designed based on the NGO's practice and expertise in TPD.

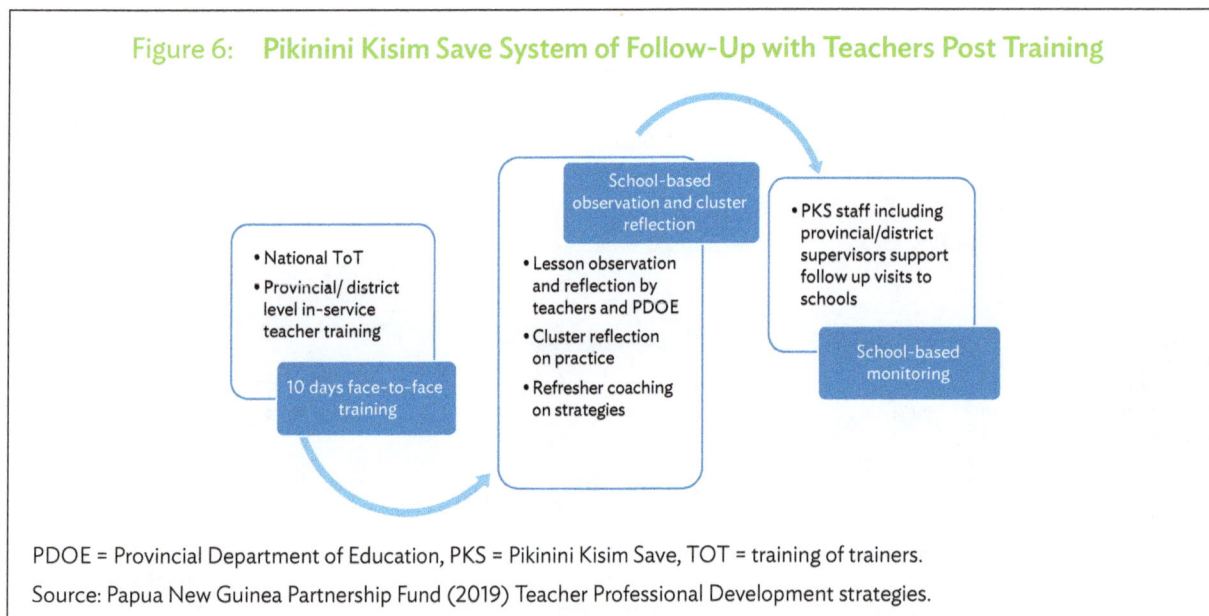

Figure 6:   **Pikinini Kisim Save System of Follow-Up with Teachers Post Training**

PDOE = Provincial Department of Education, PKS = Pikinini Kisim Save, TOT = training of trainers.

Source: Papua New Guinea Partnership Fund (2019) Teacher Professional Development strategies.

In summary, the TPD strategies (see Figure 6), were:

(i)   **Pikinini Kisim Save (PKS)**: Establishing a structure for reflection and follow-up whereby teachers from nearby villages cluster together at least two times per year to observe teachers in one school and undertake joint reflection on how they have integrated teaching strategies into their teaching practice. This is done collaboratively with provincial and district education officers. Based on teacher reflection, gaps are identified and addressed through in-situ training provided by a CARE facilitator.

(ii)   **Together for Education (T4E)**: The establishment of a comprehensive post-training monitoring schedule where teachers receive two monitoring visits annually, essentially modeling what provincial education department supervisors might do in their role. During these monitoring visits, teachers are observed, and discussions are held with teachers about changes to their teaching practices resulting from in-service training.

(iii)   **Rapidly Improving Education Standards (RISE):** The approach was twofold. The establishment of peer learning circles was driven by the teachers themselves. Oversight was provided by Save the Children education officers at the provincial level who provided guidance on the establishment of peer learning circles and supported them to plan sessions and discussion points. This was complemented by school visits to observe classes and provide feedback.

Results

While modifications to training schedules were made, the in-service teacher training component of each project was implemented as planned, with elementary teachers receiving 10–15 days of in-service teacher training annually. Teacher training was conducted through provisional and district workshops, facilitated by a mix of NGO and provincial education trainers. Each project endeavored to limit the number of cascades to two.

The post-training strategies deployed by the NGOs did, however, experience challenges during implementation. For instance, T4E was not able to complete two visits (see Figure 7) for each teacher in the first year of implementation due to delays in their training rollout and unexpected delays in developing training resources.

Figure 7:   Together for Education System of Follow-Up with Teachers Post Training

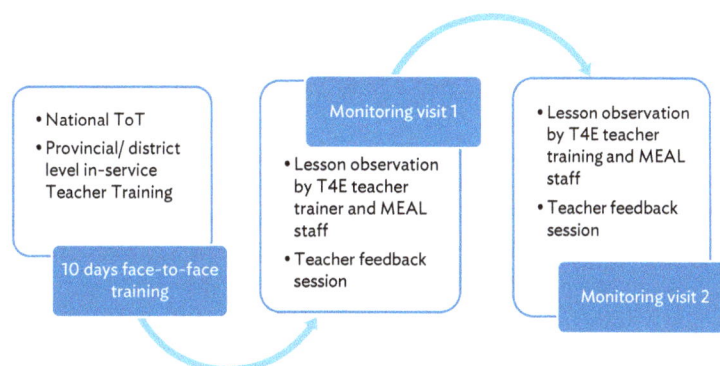

- National ToT
- Provincial/ district level in-service Teacher Training

10 days face-to-face training

Monitoring visit 1
- Lesson observation by T4E teacher trainer and MEAL staff
- Teacher feedback session

- Lesson observation by T4E teacher training and MEAL staff
- Teacher feedback session

Monitoring visit 2

MEAL = Monitoring, Evaluation, Accountability, and Learning; TOT = training of trainers; T4E = Together for Education.

Source: Papua New Guinea Partnership Fund (2019) Teacher Professional Development strategies.

RISE was unable to support the establishment of peer learning circles (PLCs) in all areas due to distance, poor road conditions, higher than anticipated transport costs, and a lack of time allocated for field monitoring. While attendance at training sessions was high, participation rates in PLCs were low and required significant support from Save the Children. The PKS project was unable to establish teacher reflection and coaching clusters in a way that would drive improvement and the approach was revised following a monitoring visit in mid-2019 to provide greater structure to the coaching sessions. Adaptations and adjustments were made in the second year and some promising post-training support strategies are emerging for school-based TPD in PNG.

Training evaluation reports have shown that teacher confidence has grown in teaching reading, basic literacy, and using the SBC. Pre- and post-tests from the PKS SBC English teacher training showed that teachers have a better

Figure 8:   Rapidly Improving Education Standards System of Follow-Up with Teachers Post Training

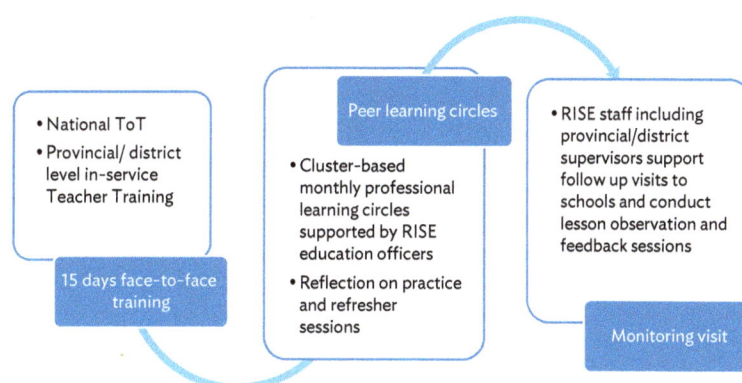

- National ToT
- Provincial/ district level in-service Teacher Training

15 days face-to-face training

Peer learning circles
- Cluster-based monthly professional learning circles supported by RISE education officers
- Reflection on practice and refresher sessions

- RISE staff including provincial/district supervisors support follow up visits to schools and conduct lesson observation and feedback sessions

Monitoring visit

RISE = Rapidly Improving Education Standards, TOT = training of trainers.

Source: Papua New Guinea Partnership Fund (2019) Teacher Professional Development strategies.

understanding of the structure of the SBC and an increased understanding of key concepts in the SBC. The report described a 28% increase in teachers who know the correct total number of phonemes; a 10% increase in the number of teachers who correctly defined what a "sight word" is; and a 20% increase in the number of teachers who know what a decodable text is. In mathematics training evaluations, teachers reported increased confidence using manipulatives to complete number operations such as addition and subtraction. Classroom monitoring data from the T4E project show that teachers were observed practicing 2–3 age-appropriate literacy and numeracy strategies in the classroom.

However, according to RISE evaluation reports, implementation of the SBC continues to be a challenge for teachers as they have not received adequate orientation from the Provincial Department of Education (PDOE). As such, teachers who are not confident in some topics or content of the SBC continue to miss or skip sessions. The RISE end line evaluation found that despite the training received, this remained a significant issue, with 41.51% of teachers in treatment schools and 56.52% of teachers in control schools missing or skipping sections of the SBC.

The post-training TPD strategies showed some promise, but are still weak. The RISE approach was perhaps the most ambitious and the least successful in the first year of implementation. PLCs were initially grouped by neighboring villages or wards within the same area. However, geographical barriers between schools in the cluster and a reluctance of teachers to share the experience with teachers from another school limited its success. The PLCs were subsequently reorganized so that teachers within the same school could hold PLCs to support and share experiences. Yet teacher attendance remained low and relied heavily on Save the Children officers to oversee the sessions. Save the Children technical staff, community education officers, and teacher trainers, however, did not have the capacity or time to support this part of the program alongside their other responsibilities. In a monitoring visit in October 2019, it was recommended that a more robust format for the sessions be developed to help guide and support teachers in conducting PLCs.

The T4E approach was successful in that monitoring visits were conducted, and that most teachers received at least two visits per year. The system at the school level to observe a teacher first and then spend time with that teacher providing feedback and offering advice follows sound logic. In practice, it was unclear whether feedback provided to teachers targeted the teaching strategies that were emphasized during training. The model may be difficult to replicate by the government because of the resource intensity of one-to-one school visits. Recommendations following monitoring (May 2019) included reviewing the lesson observation and coaching forms to ensure that teacher trainers who observe the lessons have a robust set of strategies for feedback to teachers and are supported to co-teach and/or demonstrate teaching strategies that are observed as weak.

The PKS approach possibly shows the greatest promise as it uses tools that provincial education authorities can readily adapt to and adopt and can be systematically applied. As with advice provided to T4E, recommendations following monitoring (August 2019) included strengthening the structure of coaching sessions and providing materials and resources, such as reading books for practice and stationery supplies to make teaching aids for in-situ training. The exercise to have teachers observe other teachers and then reflect collectively on what has been observed shows promise and provides a platform for shared learning. With a more structured coaching session, this seems to be a model that provides teachers with an effective mix of reflective practice and peer learning, two important ingredients of effective TPD.

Midline assessments were carried out after a full year of the training cycle. Improvements in teaching practice were evident and showed promising signs that the intervention is leading to improvements in teacher capacity to teach English and Mathematics (see Figure 8).

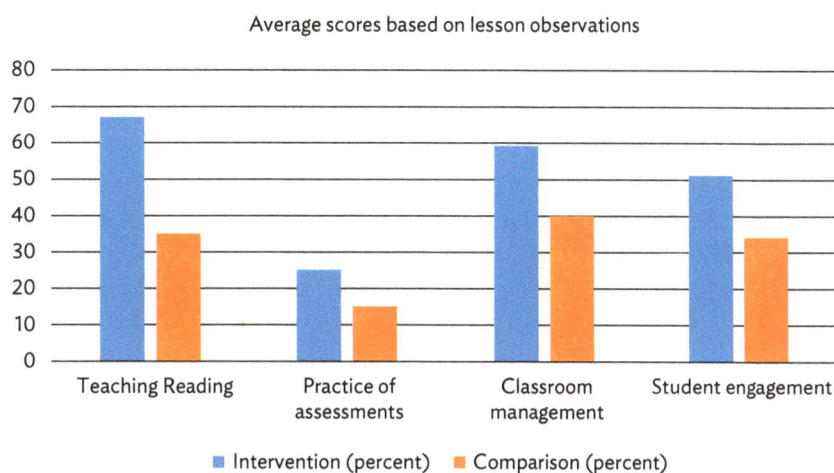

Figure 9:   Teacher Competency Scores in Intervention and Comparison Schools

Average scores based on lesson observations

Source: Papua New Guinea Partnership Fund (2020) Midline synthesis report.

To illustrate, RISE found that teachers in intervention schools scored much higher in some areas including reading comprehension, assessment, classroom management, and student engagement (Johnston et al. 2019). Figure 9 shows the percentage difference between the two teacher cohorts.

Furthermore, T4E reported that teachers from the intervention schools were more likely to:

(i)   inform students why they are learning the content;
(ii)   model how to do the work or activity;
(iii)   wrap up or summarize at the end of the lesson;
(iv)   ask questions before, during, and after reading;
(v)   give oral feedback when teaching or checking for understanding;
(vi)   give students manipulatives as learning materials during math lessons; and
(vii)   positively manage student-to-student relationships. (Simoncini et al. 2019).

Lessons

The results of the project midline assessments and evidence from monitoring visits demonstrate that while the in-service teacher training component of the projects is improving knowledge and awareness, work remains to be done to establish strong school-based post-training TPD that ensures teachers improve their practice. Seven key lessons came from the PPF funded projects:

(i)   The need to balance resources spent on face-to-face training with resources spent on follow-up to ensure post-training TPD is adequately prioritized in the implementation plan and budget.
(ii)   Adequately train and support those identified and selected as coaches or mentors to teachers. It is incumbent on the projects that coaches and mentors provide the correct advice and have the capacity to model the desired practice when required. Exemplar teachers may make the best mentors and coaches rather than supervisors or head teachers.
(iii)   Test the concept of cluster-based learning opportunities in rural settings of PNG to ensure the model is feasible and viewed as valuable by the teachers. The projects assumed that teachers would value frequent meetings, but teachers did not have time and some regions faced clan conflict and rivalry, so a meeting was not conducive outside their villages.

(iv)   Conduct a highly structured follow-up process that provides detailed guidance to trainers, teachers, mentors, head teachers—among others—so the process steps and content are fully understood by key stakeholders. There should be a balance between heavily scripted instruction and open-ended exploratory guidance.

(v)   Pay greater attention to the cascaded training, which is rolled out after the initial training of trainers to adequately support core trainers and ensure key concepts and strategies are not lost.

(vi)   Rework the concept of peer learning circles and integrate peer learning into all school-based follow-up processes like what is being further refined in the PKS project.

(vii)   Work closely with the provincial education authorities to embed the concept of continuous TPD within the provincial education system and identify roles of key education officers who can support teachers professionally. These education personnel should be engaged in the projects and provided with sufficient training to fulfill their role. The PKS project utilized PDOE elementary trainers, who may be suitable resource staff for teachers. It is often assumed that district supervisors are the best resource for teachers, but district supervisors rarely receive orientation on teaching pedagogy, subject matter specialization, and the SBC. They may be ex-teachers, but their primary role as a supervisor is to complete school checks not to give practical teaching advice to teachers.

Philippines—Early Language Literacy and Numeracy Digital

Author: Philippine Department of Education, Bureau for Learning Delivery

Background

The Department of Education (DepEd) of the Philippines formulates and implements policies and programs to ensure a "complete, adequate, and integrated system of basic education relevant to the goals of national development" (Department of Education 2020). It is organized and administered centrally by the Office of the Secretary, with undersecretaries for the offices of the Chief of Staff, Curriculum and Instruction, Planning Service and Field Operations, Administration, Finance, Legislative Affairs and External Partnerships, Operations, Employee Welfare, Personnel, and the DepEd Employees Coordinating Office. This structure provides supervision, support, and continuous professional development for over 800,000 teachers in over 60,000 schools, 223 divisions, and 17 administrative regions nationwide. This includes public, private, and Philippine schools overseas (DepEd 2019).

From 2011 to 2021, DepEd has undergone major reforms affecting teacher professional development (TPD). The 2013 Basic Education Law (Official Gazette 2013) transformed the curriculum to include 2 years of senior high school and required the utilization of a "mother tongue-based multilingual education." This was preceded by the implementation in 2011 of universal kindergarten education (DepEd 2011). In October 2014, DepEd's Every Child a Reader program launched the in-service teacher training program, Early Language Literacy and Numeracy (ELLN) for Kindergarten to Grade 3 teachers (K–3). In 2015, DepEd Order No. 12 required all K–3 teachers to possess the basic competencies covered by ELLN (DepEd 2015). In 2016, DepEd established the Learning Action Cell (LAC) as the school-based mentoring and co-learning mechanism to support TPD (DepEd 2016). In 2019, Republic Act 10912—known as the Continuous Professional Development Law, which requires teachers to earn Continuous Professional Development units to maintain their license to practice—came into full effect (Philippine Congress 2016).

Given the magnitude of TPD needs within the system, DepEd is faced with three major challenges in delivering in-service training: (i) maintaining the quality of training as it goes to scale; (ii) sustaining quality training and making it continuous; and (iii) assessing the impact of in-service training on teacher competencies and practice. For decades, the dominant model of in-service training has been the face-to-face cascade model in which regional and divisional trainers are trained by expert instructors, who then reproduce this training to teachers and school leaders. While this model enables training to scale quickly, issues of quality persist. Quality of training is constrained by training periods limited to the summer and semestral breaks, a small pool of expert trainers and facilitators especially at subnational levels, and unevenness in both access to training resources and quality of training management. The constitution of school-based LACs is a significant step in achieving continuity of teacher learning, but the effectiveness of this mechanism depends in large part on a steady flow of expert instruction and high quality content to support and sustain TPD.

Intervention

Recognizing the need for flexible, cost-effective, scalable, and sustainable models for continuing TPD, DepEd collaborated with the Foundation for Information Technology Education and Development (FIT-ED) from 2016 to 2017 to develop and test a technology-supported, blended model of TPD delivery to complement the face-to-face cascade model. Funding for the pilot was provided by the United States Agency for International Development (USAID) through the Philippine-American Fund. The parameters below for the pilot project were set by a Project Management Committee co-chaired by the director of DepEd's Bureau for Learning Delivery and FIT-ED's executive director:

(i)   The pilot course would be based on DepEd's 10-day face-to-face ELLN course for K–3 teachers.
(ii)   Pilot schools would be selected from a white list of public elementary schools that have not yet received face-to-face ELLN training or other similar training.
(iii) The blended model would not require teachers to study online as teacher access to devices and the internet is uneven across the country.
(iv)   The blended model would activate and maximize co-learning in the LAC.

The blended model that was developed for testing—called ELLN Digital—had two components: (i) guided independent study of self-study multimedia courseware, with classroom application of concepts learned; and (ii) collaborative learning in a school-based LAC (Figure 10).

A team of experts in literacy and numeracy teaching and technology-supported learning was responsible for developing the model and the pilot course. Courseware development was based on an analysis of the face-to-face ELLN instructional design and materials, as well as feedback from ELLN trainers (FIT-ED 2017). The face-to-face ELLN sessions were adapted—following principles of independent adult learning—into five modules; four on literacy and one on numeracy. These five modules included 15 lessons based on DepEd's 10-day face-to-face training course on ELLN instruction for K–3 teachers. The four literacy modules covered internationally recognized topics as important to literacy teaching in the early years of school. Supplemental information and resources were included in the courseware. Detailed guides were developed for teachers, LAC facilitators, school heads, and learning facilitators (expert coaches). DepEd reviewed and approved all course materials before pilot delivery.

The initial pilot design specified a sample of 15 K–3 teachers per pilot school (the maximum size of a LAC), and the provision of capacitation and support on facilitation and coaching directly to school-based LAC facilitators (the school head or designated teachers). DepEd chose instead to expand the pilot to include all K–3 teachers in a pilot school, and to capacitate existing division- and region-based technical assistance providers (education supervisors and master teachers trained in face-to-face ELLN) to provide expert coaching. DepEd's decision was based on the urgent need to provide all K–3 teachers with ELLN training as quickly and efficiently as possible.

Figure 10:   **Pilot Early Language Literacy and Numeracy Digital Blended Learning Teacher Professional Development Model**

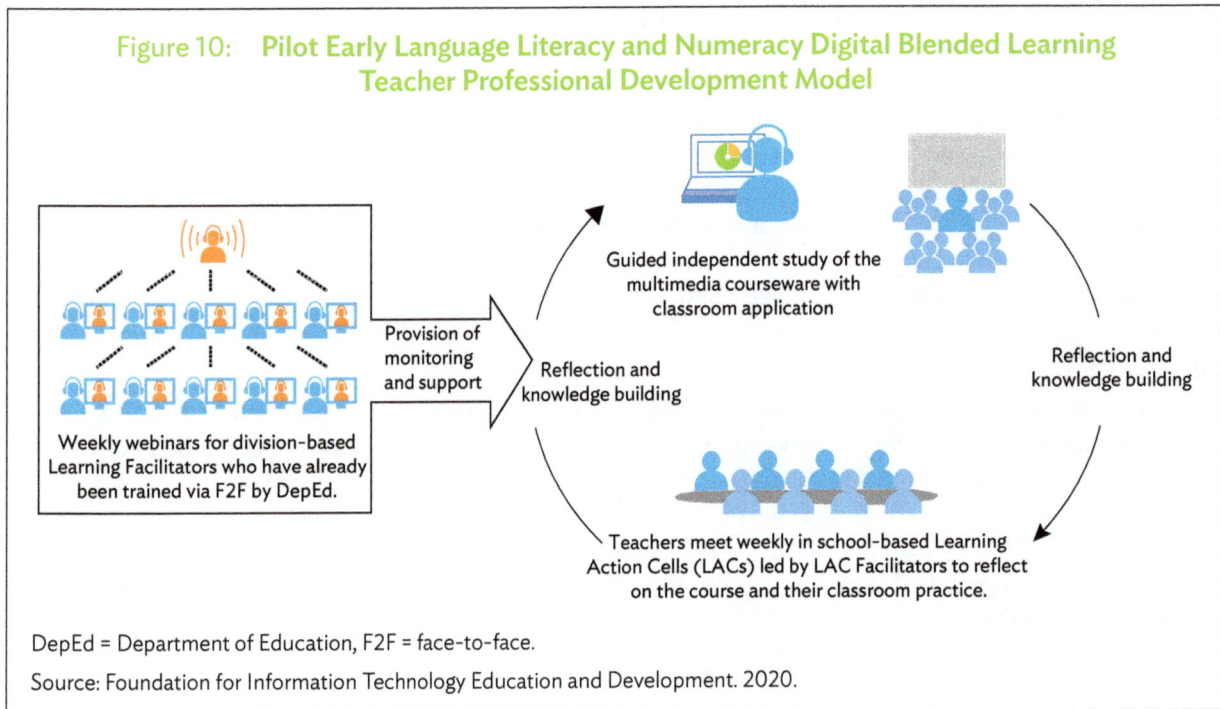

Weekly webinars for division-based Learning Facilitators who have already been trained via F2F by DepEd.

Provision of monitoring and support

Guided independent study of the multimedia courseware with classroom application

Reflection and knowledge building

Reflection and knowledge building

Teachers meet weekly in school-based Learning Action Cells (LACs) led by LAC Facilitators to reflect on the course and their classroom practice.

DepEd = Department of Education, F2F = face-to-face.

Source: Foundation for Information Technology Education and Development. 2020.

The four literacy modules of ELLN Digital were piloted over 5 months from November 2016 to March 2017 with 4,030 K–3 teachers from 240 schools in 31 divisions who had not previously taken the face-to-face ELLN or similar course. Each pilot school was given copies of the ELLN Digital courseware and guides for reproduction as well as a set of five storybooks used in the course. Schools were instructed to provide each teacher with a personal copy of the courseware. The LAC Facilitators Guide detailed how each LAC session was to be conducted. LACs were supported and monitored by 31 division- and region-based learning facilitators. These learning facilitators were given webinars on mentoring and providing mobile phones and wireless modems for communicating with the LACs regularly.

Results

Pilot teachers benefited from access to standardized expertise embedded in the courseware. This included structured discussions of key concepts, principles, approaches, and strategies; video and audio demonstrations; templates and worksheets; practical assignments; and assessment activities. Independent study and practice were reinforced by structured collegial study in the LAC. The school-based TPD was monitored and supported by learning facilitators equipped with strategies and tools for facilitating learning. At the end of the pilot, 3,848— or 95%—of the pilot teachers completed all or some of the course modules.

An impact evaluation of the pilot conducted by independent researchers from the University of Western Australia and The Education University of Hong Kong funded by the International Development Research Centre found that pilot teachers and school principals were generally positive about the course, its content, and its design.

This indicated that valuable teacher learning had occurred, which they thought was impacting on teaching practice, and, in turn, children's learning. Teachers were generally positive about the blended learning model, which combined LACs, designed to be communities of practice in which teachers discussed the courseware and reflected on their practice, with CD courseware intended to be studied before LAC meetings in a flexible, self-paced learning mode. The model was designed to encourage teachers to take charge of their learning within communities of practice. Teachers indicated that they found the LACs a safe and supportive space where they were able to reflect on and discuss their learning and practice (Oakley 2018).

To measure the impact of ELLN Digital on teachers' knowledge and skills in early literacy instruction, two tests were administered to a random sample of 434 pilot teachers before and after course delivery: a Content and Pedagogical Knowledge Test and a Teacher's Needs and Strengths Assessment. Test results showed a significant improvement in the teachers' content and pedagogical knowledge and needs and strengths assessment scores at the end of the pilot, with some variations between subgroups of teachers. Results of an end-of-course survey revealed that teachers found the courseware clear and easy to navigate, that LACs helped them learn, and that the course was both enjoyable and useful.

The evaluation also noted several issues that affected the effectiveness of ELLN Digital. First, not all teachers had sufficient access to the courseware and a computer or other classroom resources mentioned in the course such as storybooks. This constrained them from fully engaging in self-paced learning. Second, some teachers found the course content unchallenging or unrelatable, suggesting a need for more differentiated materials and activities. Third, not all LACs were implemented as intended. Some LAC facilitators gave presentation-style lectures instead of encouraging discussion, reflection, and problem-solving. Lastly, assessment of teacher learning could be strengthened through more formative assessment activities and more support for self- and peer assessment.

The courseware and guides were enhanced and supplemented based on the findings of the evaluation. ELLN Digital Version 2.0 was turned over to DepEd in August 2018 for national scale-up (TPD@Scale Coalition for the Global South 2019). The national rollout of ELLN Digital began in earnest in July 2019 via island cluster workshops for field implementers from all 223 divisions, organized by the Office of the Undersecretary for Curriculum Instruction and Development, through the Bureau of Learning Delivery, and co-facilitated with FIT-ED (Department of Education Region VI 2019). To support and sustain effective scaling, the improvement science-based Plan-Do-Study-Act approach was introduced for continuous monitoring, learning, and improvement (Figure 11).

Evaluation of the first phase of the national scale-up implementation is ongoing as of 2021. DepEd and FIT-ED are collaborating on developing more ELLN Digital support materials as well as on sourcing funds and technical

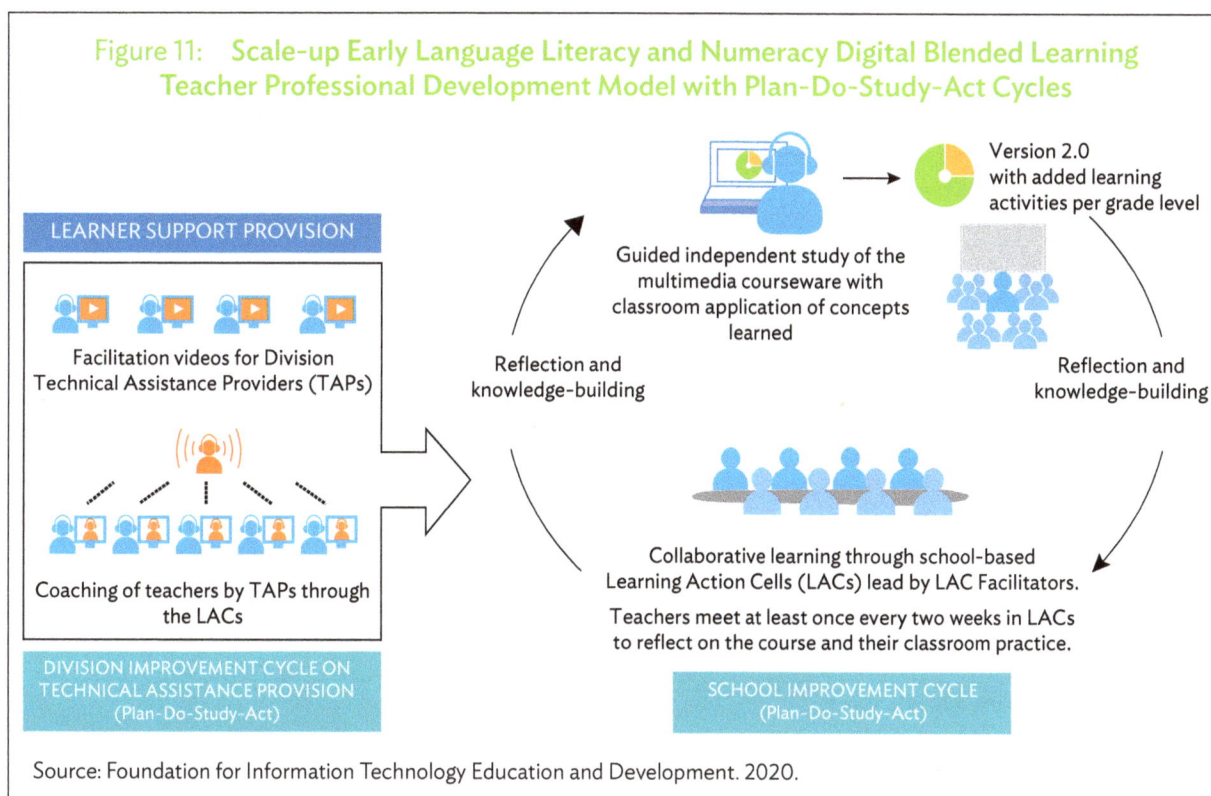

Figure 11:   Scale-up Early Language Literacy and Numeracy Digital Blended Learning Teacher Professional Development Model with Plan-Do-Study-Act Cycles

LEARNER SUPPORT PROVISION

Facilitation videos for Division Technical Assistance Providers (TAPs)

Coaching of teachers by TAPs through the LACs

DIVISION IMPROVEMENT CYCLE ON TECHNICAL ASSISTANCE PROVISION (Plan-Do-Study-Act)

Guided independent study of the multimedia courseware with classroom application of concepts learned

Version 2.0 with added learning activities per grade level

Reflection and knowledge-building

Reflection and knowledge-building

Collaborative learning through school-based Learning Action Cells (LACs) lead by LAC Facilitators.

Teachers meet at least once every two weeks in LACs to reflect on the course and their classroom practice.

SCHOOL IMPROVEMENT CYCLE (Plan-Do-Study-Act)

Source: Foundation for Information Technology Education and Development. 2020.

assistance for developing and testing more courseware for other learning areas and year levels, and for mentoring DepEd national, regional, and division trainers. It is notable that since the enforcement of school closures and community lockdowns in March 2020 due to the COVID-19 pandemic, some divisions have reported continued implementation of ELLN Digital. Whatever the "new normal" may be post-COVID-19, DepEd will work toward implementing the blended TPD model across the K–12 curriculum and—if successful—envisions that this innovation will have a deep and far-reaching impact on the quality of basic education in the Philippines.

Lessons

The ELLN Digital pilot was demand-driven from the outset. DepEd's TPD priorities, needs, and operational contexts determined targets and informed model development and pilot implementation. FIT-ED was tasked to leverage and strengthen existing DepEd systems and capacities, where and when possible, and create opportunities and affordances where it was not.

Project buy-in at all levels of DepEd was pivotal to the success of the pilot. Division- and school-level management commitment is required, with support from the regional office, for the blended TPD model to be viable. Central Office buy-in is essential for institutionalization and scale-up.

The pilot also confirmed the need for a lengthy period of coordination with DepEd before project implementation and sufficient lead time for preparation at field levels, given the complexities of DepEd's operations.

Finally, as the independent evaluation of the pilot concludes, the effectiveness of the blended TPD model can only be maximized if the model is enacted as intended. This entails ensuring that teachers and school leaders

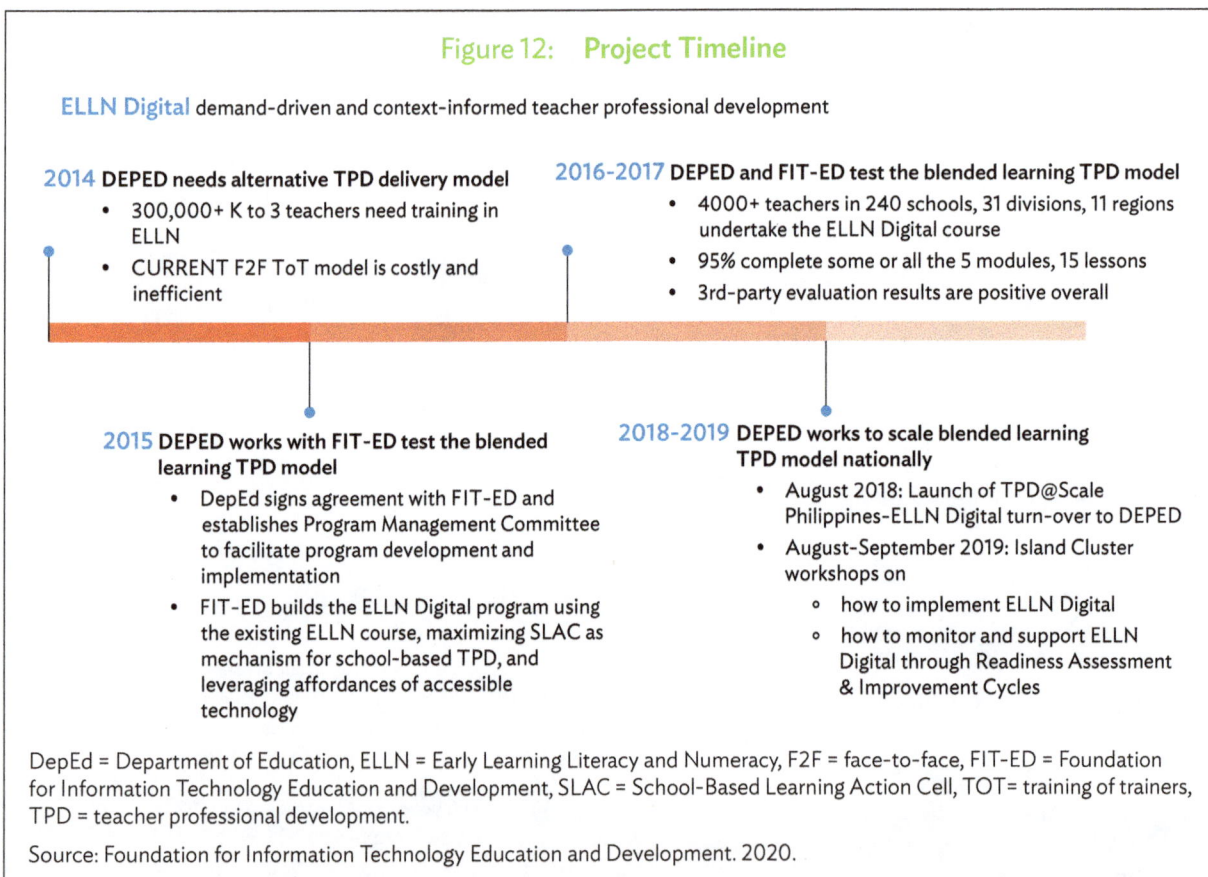

Figure 12:   Project Timeline

ELLN Digital demand-driven and context-informed teacher professional development

2014 DEPED needs alternative TPD delivery model
- 300,000+ K to 3 teachers need training in ELLN
- CURRENT F2F ToT model is costly and inefficient

2016-2017 DEPED and FIT-ED test the blended learning TPD model
- 4000+ teachers in 240 schools, 31 divisions, 11 regions undertake the ELLN Digital course
- 95% complete some or all the 5 modules, 15 lessons
- 3rd-party evaluation results are positive overall

2015 DEPED works with FIT-ED test the blended learning TPD model
- DepEd signs agreement with FIT-ED and establishes Program Management Committee to facilitate program development and implementation
- FIT-ED builds the ELLN Digital program using the existing ELLN course, maximizing SLAC as mechanism for school-based TPD, and leveraging affordances of accessible technology

2018-2019 DEPED works to scale blended learning TPD model nationally
- August 2018: Launch of TPD@Scale Philippines-ELLN Digital turn-over to DEPED
- August-September 2019: Island Cluster workshops on
  - how to implement ELLN Digital
  - how to monitor and support ELLN Digital through Readiness Assessment & Improvement Cycles

DepEd = Department of Education, ELLN = Early Learning Literacy and Numeracy, F2F = face-to-face, FIT-ED = Foundation for Information Technology Education and Development, SLAC = School-Based Learning Action Cell, TOT= training of trainers, TPD = teacher professional development.

Source: Foundation for Information Technology Education and Development. 2020.

understand how the model works and all the resources necessary for the model to work are made available to teachers in a timely way (see Figure 12 for the project timeline).

Timor-Leste—Systemic Approaches to Supporting Teacher's Skills

Authors: Ester Correia, Peter Grimes, Antonina Marques, and Almanzo Salsinha

Background
Timor-Leste has made significant gains in education since its independence. School enrollments have rapidly increased, with girls' rates exceeding boys' rates at each level of schooling. In 2010, 94% of primary school age girls and 92% of boys were enrolled in school (ADB Timor-Leste Gender Assessment 2014). This is supported by strong government policies and legislative frameworks, including the National Education Strategic Plan and Strategic Development Plan.

However, significant challenges remain. Data from 2011 indicate that few children had acquired basic skills—such as literacy and numeracy—by the time they completed their early grades of schooling. For example; in 2011, only 3% of Grade 1 students attained an average fluency of 45 correct words per minute, only 21% were able to answer simple addition, and only 12% answered simple subtraction questions correctly (World Bank, .EGRA [Early Grade Reading Assessment], and EGMA [Early Grade Mathematics Assessment] 2011).

There have also been challenges in teachers' skills, knowledge, and qualification (71% of primary school teachers and 51% of primary school directors have only completed high school). School leaders have mostly either been focusing on administration or are still teaching a class themselves. They find it difficult to support their teachers' ability to improve pedagogy, as many leaders themselves do not have the pedagogic skills nor the curriculum content knowledge required to implement the new curriculum.

Intervention
In response to these challenges, in 2013, the Timor-Leste Ministry of Education, Youth and Sports (MoEYS) began a staged development of a new curriculum for preschool to Grade 6, to improve literacy and numeracy. The new National Basic Education Curriculum organizes subject content into sequenced and scripted lessons for each grade level to support teachers to implement the new curriculum, and to ensure content uniformity across classes and schools. It also utilizes new pedagogies that aim to transform teaching and learning approaches in Timor-Leste, moving from traditional teacher-centered approaches to student-centered ones.

To ensure that basic education school leaders and teachers implement the new national curriculum effectively, in 2015, the Government of Australia worked with MoEYS to support the design and implementation of the Professional Learning and Mentoring Program (ALMA). This was established to build school leadership and teacher capacity to improve teaching practice and student learning in Grades 1 to 6. School leaders and teachers are provided with ongoing professional development support in the school environment to implement the MoEYS national curriculum and to teach using student-centered methodologies. At the same time, ALMA has been working with MoEYS to strengthen key government systems to support the effective planning and delivery of quality education.

ALMA has been implemented in phases: implementation runs for 9 to 12 months, and consolidation runs for 6 months to support the sustainability of ALMA activities. ALMA continues to support schools from each phase through school inspector visits and—as of 2019—through newly established systems and personnel in municipal education offices. ALMA activities—such as classroom observation and monitoring, literacy and numeracy assessments, and school-based in-service teacher development sessions—are transitioned to school inspectors, with support and supervision from auditors, Basic Education offices, and the national in-service teacher training institution. These actors are also supported through the establishment of systems and technology to monitor and report on their activities in schools, such as classroom observation forms, or tablets.

The ALMA program includes the following core components:

(i) **Leaders of Learning Program**. School leaders attend a series of four 2-day leadership training sessions on topics such as school-based management, observation, and feedback skills, provision of teacher support, literacy and numeracy assessment, teacher peer learning groups, inclusive education, intensive literacy sessions for teachers, and parent-community involvement in schools. The training sessions are held 3 to 4 months apart.

(ii) **School-based peer professional learning groups**. School leaders and teachers teaching in the same grade level in a school cluster meet regularly to work together and learn from each other by planning lessons together, providing feedback to each other, discussing resources and problem-solving issues in teaching and learning.

(iii) **Mentor support from educational and local mentors.** A team of international and national education mentors provides on-the-job mentoring to school leaders as they apply the learning gained from the leadership training. Mentors also support teacher capacity through peer learning groups, providing classroom observation and feedback sessions, conducting student literacy and numeracy assessments, and supporting intensive literacy sessions for teachers. The mentors have extensive experience and training in education and specialization in areas such as school leadership, literacy and numeracy, professional learning, special education, and disabilities in school. Education mentors work closely with the National Mentor from MoEYS and local mentors who have education experience and qualifications.

(iv) **Education technology to enable efficient information sharing and monitoring**. The use of technology enables the program to share information, monitor, and evaluate its progress and engage in peer-to-peer networking. School leaders are given a tablet with custom-built apps and a dashboard to collect, store and submit classroom observation data, as well as to retrieve and analyze information. Each tablet is uploaded with the new curriculum, lesson plans, and materials. Tablets also allow school leaders to film classes, provide feedback, and watch motivational and good practice videos.

ALMA was developed in partnership by Australia and MoEYS, with contributions provided by the governments of Timor-Leste and Australia. The program is now a government program delivered by MoEYS government staff, with support from the Australia-Timor-Leste Partnership for Human Development. As of 2020, ALMA has been rolled out in 10 of the 13 municipalities of Timor-Leste. Recent ALMA program updates include (i) a greater focus on embedding inclusion and equity across all aspects of the program; (ii) strengthening government systems to improve effectiveness (such as human resources, environment management information systems, and monitoring and evaluation systems [M&E], curriculum distribution, teacher development approaches and strategies, and use of ICT within MoEYS); (iii) refresher training for school leaders in all municipalities; (iv) updates to teacher observation forms to align them to teacher competency frameworks; and, (v) chat groups on the school leaders' tablets.

Result

The capacity and commitment of school leaders are critical to improving the quality of teaching and learning in schools. The ALMA program consistently analyzes its effectiveness and adapts to respond flexibly to the needs of basic education school leaders and teachers. In 2020, there was strong evidence that school leaders' capacity and performance improved across all domains that ALMA aims to influence, including classroom observation, providing feedback and counseling, reporting, use of technology, as well as attitudes or role modeling.

The establishment of a more rigorous and reliable M&E system for the program (Program-Based Inquiry) was introduced in 2019 to support monitoring by tracking leaders' and teachers' progress and students' learning outcomes.

The mentoring criteria for classroom observation require the leader to remain focused on the classroom dynamics and not interfere, to understand the lesson plan that he or she is observing, and to write down both positive and negative observations. Internal program monitoring shows that there was a significant improvement in school leaders' performance in Lautem against the "curriculum" criteria from 50% to 70%, and "diagnosis" criteria from 40% to 55%.

A 2019 evaluation undertaken by the Australian Council for Educational Research found that ALMA is effective in empowering school leaders to support teachers through feedback and observation. Examples of feedback include:

"...the coordinators are now conducting the observation in the classrooms, which has given a good impact. In the past, they did not care about the classroom." (Municipal MoEYS, Viqueque)

"...teaching is centred on the students...active participation of the students. So while we're doing monitoring we're looking at these things." (School Leader, Bobonaro).

Teachers and leaders have identified the cluster and school-based teacher development group (GTP) as an important source of information and motivation. The school leaders' facilitation of GTPs in their clusters is an important element to create a supportive environment for teacher professional development. In Lautem, GTP activities did not start until April 2019. During that month, only two GTPs were conducted by two of 15 clusters across the whole municipality. By November 2019, 75 GTPs had been conducted across all 15 clusters. Across the whole ALMA program, 190 GTP sessions were conducted during this period by school leaders at the cluster level to enhance teachers' skills and develop capacity. The GTP sessions covered topics such as preparation and implementation of lesson plans (26%), assessment and evaluation (15%), and content of lesson plans (14%).

The Australian Council for Educational Research report (2019) found that "ALMA is effective in supporting implementation of the National Basic Education Curriculum through facilitating a peer learning process for teachers to prepare, review and present lessons, provide feedback, share challenges and workshop solutions. It is also effective in supporting teachers and school leaders to utilize and access lesson plans and materials." This was supported by teachers' comments on the importance of the GTPs:

"GTP always helps, whatever challenges we face in our teaching period and we cannot solve them alone, through GTP we can do it together. A teacher has an issue then we will solve them together. That's what's good from GTP." (Teacher, Bobonaro)

"If we are really facing a problem, then we can start to understand it at the GTP. Because all the schools come together, so there are teachers with more experience than us and they can explain it clearly." (Teacher, Bobonaro)

Lessons and Challenges

The success of the program appears to be based on its evidence-informed approach to sustainable teacher development. Leaders and teachers are supported through mentoring by government and program actors to make small changes to their practice that are achievable and not overwhelming. Reflective needs analysis then takes place, which leads to further changes in practice, and which are supported through targeted school- and cluster-based teacher development activity. Leadership training of all leaders in schools reinforces the key approaches and principles.

The program gives leaders the support and space to respond flexibly to the needs and requirements of the teachers in their context and notes that these contexts may be different in certain locations influenced by barriers such as:

    (i)   remote geography,

    (ii)   economic hardship including poor nutrition leading to stunting in young children,

    (iii)   attitudes toward gender and disability,

    (iv)   challenges with teachers, and

    (v)   children's experience of the language of instruction.

Where ongoing support is provided, both leaders and teachers are demonstrating that this has a positive impact on their practice resulting in improved learning outcomes for children.

Successful implementation of ALMA requires additional focus on systems strengthening for sustainability. Any program aiming to improve teacher performance needs to take this into account and pay attention to a wide range of factors. Innovation without systemic strengthening seems unlikely to be sustainable.

Implementation of ALMA is still highly dependent on development partners to coordinate and provide leadership and strategic direction. A gradual process of supported transition is enabling the government to become more involved in the day-to-day running of the program and the school improvement processes which ALMA enables. For example, environmental management information systems and M&E are being strengthened to enable municipal education offices to monitor school data, identify strengths and weaknesses, and then intervene with weaker schools that need further support.

Teacher performance data needs to be made easily accessible to different actors throughout the system through IT. This includes developing a new education portal allowing those in leadership roles at all levels of the system to track and analyze data that can inform their strategic responses.

Schools that were introduced to ALMA in the first years of the program require significant support to continue to follow the program. Similarly, several schools have not been included so far in the program, and these need to be gradually introduced.

The government needs to gradually take on responsibility for budget allocation to support program implementation to ensure that functionalities are embedded in the education system and are directly managed through the government.

Ghana—Transforming Teacher Education and Learning

Author: Robin Todd, Team Leader, Cambridge Education

Background

Public Colleges of Education (CoEs) lie at the heart of Ghana's initial teacher education system. In 2012, an Act of Parliament (Colleges of Education) upgraded these institutions to tertiary status. The responsibility for oversight and performance of teacher education passed from the Ghana Education Service to the National Council for Tertiary Education (NCTE). The Pre-Tertiary Teacher Professional Development and Management Framework set out a holistic ambition for teacher development, management, and performance within Ghana.

Dedicated national agencies such as the National Teaching Council (NTC), National Inspectorate Board, and the National Council for Curriculum and Assessment were established to help the teacher education system address the poor learning outcomes recorded across Ghana's basic schools.

As of early 2014, the issues faced within CoEs were like those of a decade earlier despite these new policy developments (Akyeampong 2003; Department for International Development [DFID] 2012; Cambridge Education 2014). Major constraints to effective initial teacher education include:

(i) **Poor quality of entrants and the consequent focus on remedial content.** The 3-year Diploma in Basic Education (DBE) attracted applicants who did not have the required grades to enter university. The academic content knowledge of these applicants was generally poor—particularly in English, Mathematics, and Science—necessitating tutors for remedial lessons.

(ii) **Content-heavy and examination-oriented DBE curriculum.** This lent itself to rote learning by student-teachers.[1] Tutors predominantly used the lecture method of instruction. There was little explicit link between the content of the curriculum and the primary and secondary curriculum that student-teachers were expected to teach in basic schools.

(iii) **Lack of practical exposure to teaching.** Student-teachers gain hands-on teaching experience during their third practicum year, where they spend an extended amount of time across two semesters in partner schools. The quality of mentoring and supervision within these partner schools was variable. Tutors did not consider some teachers as adequate role models. There was often no formal oversight agreement of roles and responsibilities between the district, metropolitan, and municipal education offices, which oversee basic schools, and the CoE.

(iv) **Lack of specialization.** Along with the content-heavy nature of the curriculum, lack of specialization meant that tutors had difficulty in preparing teachers who might on the one hand be teaching reading to Primary 1 or who could be teaching English Literature to Junior High School 3.

(v) **Limited resources and lack of appropriate policies and procedures of CoEs.** Quality assurance, management, and assessment processes within institutions were often inadequate and the quality of teaching and learning was variable. Many tutors lacked the required academic qualifications to teach at the tertiary level. This combination of factors meant that CoEs were tertiary in name only.

The combined impact of these factors meant that "Teachers coming through Ghana's Colleges of Education (CoE) have limited hands-on practical exposure to good teaching methodology and fall back on familiar rote-learning" (DFID 2012).

Intervention

The Government of Ghana—with support from UK aid—designed the £25 million 6-year Transforming Teacher Education and Learning (T-TEL) program to address these persistent issues in the teacher education system. One of the central premises of T-TEL—which is implemented by Cambridge Education—was that many earlier donor-funded education improvement projects in Ghana had failed to make a lasting impact in changing behaviors and attitudes.[2] Ideas and teaching methodologies, which were successfully adopted during these projects' lifespan often faded after they had finished. This could be a result of project design and failure to either attempt underlying structural or institutional reform or to systemize changes.

---

[1] For the purposes of this case study "student-teachers" are the young people in training in the Colleges of Education who will become teachers when they graduate, "tutors" are the staff in the COEs who are responsible for training the student-teachers, "teachers" are what the student-teachers become once they have graduated and start working in basic schools. The term "teachers" is also used to describe the teachers working in partner schools who play the role of mentors to the student-teachers during the practical, classroom-based elements of their training.

[2] Examples included in the original T-TEL technical proposal include the DFID/ODA funded Junior Secondary Support to Teacher Education Project (JuSSTEP, 1989–1993) and the Support to Teacher Education Project (STEP) (1993–1997), although many more projects and programs could be cited to evidence this point.

Ghana's teacher education system in 2020 was almost unrecognizable from the situation in 2014. However, the full extent of these changes was not envisaged at the start of the program. Instead, T-TEL's original design envisaged a holistic package of activities focused predominantly within CoEs, a modest adjustment of the teacher education curriculum, and strengthening of the CoEs to make them more effective institutions.

The national and inclusive consultative process that T-TEL initiated in the teacher education community in 2016 as part of a process (the "big conversation") to mobilize a coalition for change, was the genesis of far-reaching and fundamental reforms. The "big conversation" was a series of national and regional consultations led by the National Council for Tertiary Education (NCTE) and NTC, involving participants from across the teacher education system including universities, CoEs, unions, government agencies, and civil society organizations. This process led to the production of the National Teachers' Standards (NTS), which sets out a common expectation of Ghanaian teachers' knowledge, behavior, and practice.

The NTS provided the foundation for subsequent reforms as they established a common set of agreed requirements. It defined what a "good" teacher in Ghana would be across three domains: professional values and attitudes, professional knowledge, and professional practice. This provided a basis for setting standards for teacher performance and teacher education. The NTS formed the foundation for teacher licensing, which was introduced for all new entrants to the teaching profession in 2018 and formed the basis of a review and revision of the DBE teacher education curriculum.

This review of the existing teacher education curriculum concluded that the curriculum did not provide the necessary training for beginning teachers in meeting the requirements of the NTS. The minister of education, Matthew Opoku Prempeh, then decided to replace the DBE with a new Bachelor of Education (B.Ed.) degree in Initial Teacher Education, which was to become the new minimum qualification for anyone aspiring to enter the teaching profession.

The consultative process that had been used to develop the NTS was extended to develop a National Teacher Education Curriculum Framework (NTECF). The NTECF set out the mandatory requirements which any B.Ed. in Initial Teacher Education would need to meet to be accredited by the National Accreditation Board. The NTECF required specializations for Early Grade (KG–P3), Upper Primary (P3–P6), and Junior High School (JHS1–3).

Furthermore, the Cabinet Memorandum on Policy on Teacher Education Reform—which was approved by the Cabinet of the Republic of Ghana on 28 September 2017—provided for:

(i) the official introduction of NTS for pre-service teachers;
(ii) the official introduction of the NTECF;
(iii) the proposed conversion of CoEs into university colleges, affiliated to five public universities offering teacher education curricula; and
(iv) the design of a new 4-year B.Ed. curriculum for Initial Teacher Education to be offered at the university CoEs.

T-TEL's mandate then evolved to one of supporting the NCTE to deliver this ambitious set of reforms. T-TEL achieved this by working with a team of experts to help revise the curriculum, and through support provided to all 46 CoEs through five zonal teams of education advisers. Since October 2018, Ghana's 46 public CoEs have been delivering the new B.Ed. in Initial Teacher Education, which has been carefully designed to ensure that it produces a cadre of skilled, knowledgeable, and motivated Ghanaian teachers who meet the requirements of the NTS. A team of international assessors has described the content of this B.Ed.—which was written in collaboration with a team of 105 Ghanaian educators—as being "truly world-class."

Each of the CoEs is affiliated with one of five mentoring universities that provide guidance and support and operate weekly professional development and learning sessions for tutors. The new B.Ed. curriculum blends content and pedagogy so that all tutors model the behavior and practices expected of teachers in basic school classrooms while teaching student teachers. Assessments also now focus on Supported Teaching in School (teaching practice in partner schools), continuous assessment, and portfolio building rather than on final written examinations.

Specific aspects of T-TEL's support that have helped to deliver results include:

(i) **Weekly professional development sessions in all 46 CoEs.** Tutors facilitate these, which are structured around a set of materials and handbooks co-created by writing teams of tutors and T-TEL staff. These weekly sessions are a key behavior change mechanism and attendance rates are high (average of 85% across all CoEs in 2019–2020). There is no financial incentive for attending these sessions, but participants receive certificates from NTC and NCTE, which can be used for their portfolios. T-TEL initially hired international experts to develop materials for these sessions but gradually shifted toward the use of local expertise to facilitate genuine co-creation, promote ownership of materials, and ensure their relevance.

(ii) **Autonomy of institutions.** One of T-TEL's main aims was to create a teacher education system in which the 46 public CoEs could operate as high-performing autonomous institutions that solved problems and improved learning outcomes without external assistance. There was, therefore, a strong focus on leadership development and training for principals, leadership teams, and governing councils. This was accompanied by a concerted effort to support CoEs to develop College Improvement Plans and a comprehensive set of policies aligned with national standards in areas such as assessment, information and communication technology (ICT), school partnerships, and gender equality and social inclusion.

(iii) **Payment-by-Results**. T-TEL used payment-by-results (PBR) as a mechanism to incentivize CoEs to achieve targets and objectives in their College Improvement Plans: payment after agreed results have been achieved. Funds could be used flexibly by CoEs to address teaching and learning issues. This approach proved successful and also promoted cross-learning and the sharing of good practices among CoEs. The PBR approach was extended to help incentivize the implementation of Gender Responsive Improvement Plans and curriculum delivery through the Transition Support Fund, which helped tutors upgrade their qualifications to meet tertiary standards.

Results

The teacher education reforms are driven by a desire to ensure that Ghana produces teachers who can inspire learners and encourage critical thinking, problem solving, and creativity rather than simply focusing on factual recall to pass written examinations.

While the current batch of B.Ed. student teachers will not enter basic school classrooms until 2023, the T-TEL-initiated changes in teacher education have already achieved impressive results. The most recent annual external evaluation survey—carried out in June 2019—showed that (JMK Consulting Group, 2019):

(i) The proportion of English, Science, and Mathematics tutors in CoEs demonstrating student-focused teaching methods increased from 26% in 2015 to 78% in 2019.

(ii) The proportion of English, Science, and Mathematics tutors demonstrating gender-sensitive instructional methods increased from 2% in 2015 to 80% in 2019.

These changes in the CoEs have significant and measurable impacts on the performance and behavior of newly qualified teachers in Ghana. An external survey of teaching practices among over 500 beginning teachers (those in their first year after completing training) found that:

(i)   The proportion of beginning English, Science, and Mathematics teachers with core competencies in the Pre-tertiary Teacher Professional Development and Management Policy Framework increased from 2% in 2015 to 41% in 2019.

(ii)   The proportion of beginning male and female English, Science, and Mathematics teachers demonstrating gender-responsive instructional strategies increased from <1% in 2015 to 31% in 2019.

These are impressive achievements that demonstrate the enormous improvements that have already been made in Ghana's pre-service teacher education system, largely been driven by tutors themselves through weekly professional development sessions. Now that the five universities have taken over responsibility for operating these sessions (supported by T-TEL for the 2019–2020 academic year), it is highly likely that this approach will be sustained beyond the lifespan of T-TEL, which ended in December 2020.

Lessons
The key lessons learned through T-TEL are as follows:

(i)   **Building stakeholder consensus through dialogue and consultation** with key actors and agencies across the education system to develop a shared understanding of issues.

(ii)   **Working with stakeholders to leverage this shared understanding** to produce national standards and frameworks (NTS and NTECF) approved by the Cabinet of the Republic of Ghana—the highest authority in the country—to ensure that the foundations for the teacher education reforms are binding and cannot easily be reversed or altered. These documents must have sufficient force, weight, and clarity to convince the entire education system that change is compulsory and not optional.

(iii) **Ensuring that these standards, frameworks, and related policy documents introduce strong systemic incentives** for sustained behavior change aligned with the intent of the reforms. This includes the importance of changing the assessment system so that there is a systemic incentive to move away from rote learning, written examinations, and factual recall. Changing the curriculum and introducing new methodologies and approaches will only succeed and be sustained if assessment systems are redesigned to reinforce these changes.

(iv)   **Reducing the prevalence and significance of final written examinations**, as specified in the National Teacher Education Assessment Policy (thus incentivizing more practical applied teaching and learning in CoEs) and the Quality Assurance, Accreditation, and Assessment Instrument, which enhances the focus on training and learning assessment and leadership and management when assessing the quality of CoEs.

(v)   **Introducing a program of capacity building and support for key national agencies** whose policies and actions will—to a large extent—determine the extent to which teacher education reforms improve learning outcomes in basic schools. These agencies include NCTE, NTC, the National Accreditation Board, and the National Council for Curriculum and Assessment. By providing flexible funding to enable these agencies to implement priority activities T-TEL has helped to address systemic issues that had the potential to undermine reforms if not implemented effectively (examples include teacher licensing, CoE inspection, and accreditation arrangements and the introduction of the new pre-tertiary curriculum).

(vi)   **Developing the teacher education curriculum with the pre-tertiary education curriculum** (which was rolled out to all basic schools in Ghana in September 2019) rather than seeing them as two separate processes. Developing them in conjunction will help to ensure that the content and pedagogy being learned by the teachers is harmonized with that which they will be expected to deliver in schools.

(vii)   **Enhancing the role of five public teaching universities in implementing the teacher education reforms** to introduce competition, collaboration, and incentives to invest and improve performance in CoEs. When all CoEs were overseen by a single university, there was little incentive to improve performance as that university controlled the entire system. This also meant that expertise within the other four universities was not contributing effectively to teacher education. Now that the 46 CoEs are allocated to one of five universities, this has both widened the pool of expertise available to support teacher education (from one university to five) and created incentives for each university to invest in the professional development, infrastructure, and performance oversight of their affiliated CoEs so that they compare favorably with their peers.

(viii) **Ensuring that key activities, such as weekly Tutor Professional Development sessions, take place within CoEs** and are facilitated by tutors themselves. This enhances the chance that these activities will be sustained as no one is being paid an allowance to attend, there are no external facilitators who require payment and there is no need to transport participants away from their place of work.

(ix)   **Increasing the use of Ghanaian expertise and expertise from within existing teacher education institutions** (universities and CoEs) to develop key reform materials and policies rather than reliance on international experts. This helps to ensure that there is a cadre of talented Ghanaian individuals across the country who understand the reforms and who can advocate for their continued implementation once T-TEL has ended.

(x)   **Working to build the capacity and capability of CoE leadership teams and councils** and respecting their institutional autonomy to decide how to make use of PBR funds to meet their local priorities. This has helped to ensure that funds have been used effectively to meet local needs as well as strengthening the experience and confidence of CoEs to address issues and concerns.

(xi)   **Strengthening engagement and collaboration between CoEs and municipal, metropolitan, and district directorates of education** through memorandums of understanding guiding work in partner schools. Engagement with the Ghana Education Service at a national level has proved difficult so an alternative strategy has been pursued whereby CoEs are supported to build relationships with their local education offices to strengthen collaboration and effective implementation of supported teaching in schools in partner schools.

(xii)   **Supporting existing institutions within the education system** to own and drive changes rather than establishing parallel delivery systems. The role of a program like T-TEL should be to create a trusted support and challenge function that is responsive and performance oriented and which aims to work collaboratively over time to change behavior and practices rather than seeking to implement these changes ourselves.

(xiii) **Recognizing that gender equality and social inclusion can be achieved** even in rigid cultural settings when stakeholders are properly engaged and equipped with requisite skills and resources.

Finally, one area where further work is required is in partner schools. While there is evidence of impact within CoEs, surveys show that only about 30% of mentors in the 2,500 partner schools were carrying out their roles effectively when surveyed in June 2019. However, restructuring of the supported teaching in schools (where under the new B.Ed. student teachers visit partner schools 1 day a week throughout Year 1 and Year 2) is starting to have an important impact on behavior. These regular visits from B.Ed. students, who then give feedback on the lessons they observed—if done correctly—ensures that teachers need to plan and deliver high quality lessons. The student teachers (and their tutors) are thus helping to play a regular quality assurance and external support function, which did not exist in the same way under the DBE with its in-in-out structure.

Ukraine—Teaching the Ukrainian Language for National Minorities: Approaches in Improving In-Service Training Systems

Authors: Ihor Khvorostianyi, Language Advisor; Oksana Nesterova, Project Officer; Arto Vaahtokari, Chief Technical Advisor, Finland's Support to the Ukrainian School Reform, Finnish Consulting Group

Background

Gaining its independence from the former Soviet Union in 1991, Ukraine is an Eastern European country with a declining population of 41.9 million in 2019 (State Statistics Service of Ukraine 2019). The estimated percentage of national minorities in the country is 9.4%, including 6.3% citizens of Russian national minority, and 3.1% citizens of all the rest national minorities. While a strong revitalization of the Ukrainian language started with independence, Ukraine is a true melting pot of peoples and languages. It is a multilingual, multiethnic country with a long history of regional conquests and migrations.

Since its independence in 1991, Ukraine has had wide-ranging reforms spurred by the Euromaidan Revolution in 2014. This led to a reorientation toward European integration and rhetoric support of wide-reaching social and economic reforms. The annexation of the Crimean Peninsula and protracted armed conflict in Eastern Ukraine that erupted in 2014 led to the internal dislocation of over 1 million people and ceaseless political and macroeconomic instability. Despite this, the window of opportunity for the continuation of the reforms is open, as policy makers continue to express willingness to tackle pressing challenges faced by the country (World Bank 2016).

In this context, Ukrainian education has been facing multiple challenges that risk impeding not only economic development, but also social cohesion in the country. Challenges include insufficient quality and outdated relevance of education content, teaching methods, and materials—hindering student learning outcomes—and widespread system inefficiency. Moreover, educational inequity in education quality and/or participation is more prevalent in (linguistic) minority communities.

In July 2018, a 4-year collaborative education project "Learning Together" started between Ukraine and Finland, which was joined by the European Union (EU) in late 2018. Total support for Ukrainian education is €8 million and the project is scheduled to last until July 2022. The project is being implemented by Finnish Consulting Group International. The EU is providing support to enhance instruction of the Ukrainian language as a second language (L2) among national minorities. This is in line with the Road Map of 2018 by the Ministry of Education and Science of Ukraine (MoES) for implementation of the newly adopted Education Law of Ukraine. Although the project has national coverage, the support for enhancing the Ukrainian language instruction focuses mainly on the Chernivtsi and Transcarpathian regions, where Hungarian and Romanian national minorities densely reside.

According to the MoES, 72 schools use Hungarian as the language of instruction, of which 27 schools use Hungarian and Ukrainian as languages of instruction (16,845 students). Sixty-eight schools use Romanian as the language of instruction of which 20 schools use Ukrainian and Romanian as the languages of instruction (16,109 students). None of these schools provide students with enough Ukrainian language proficiency to enter tertiary education in Ukraine. A high percentage of school graduates are failing independent evaluation tests in Ukrainian language and literature, which are integral components for admission to further education in Ukraine. These low results come from years of inflexible teaching practices (with no regard to student mother tongue), low-quality teaching materials, and limited interest from national minorities to study the Ukrainian language.

Intervention

The structure of teacher education in Ukraine hardly changed after independence in 1991, and the pedagogy in teacher training programs tended to reinforce the "transmission"—or passive—learning model. This led to the conclusion that language teaching methods had not evolved. Conventional teacher education in general has been shown in many cases to have little impact on teacher further learning or subsequent classroom instruction. The improvement of the in-service teacher training in Ukraine is urgent, as the current system cannot respond to rapid education changes and teacher needs. Effective implementation of competence-based curricula, for example, requires that teachers be prepared not only for new curriculum content-but also for a new approach to teaching and the role of the teacher as partner and facilitator.

With the new Education Law of 2017, the Government of Ukraine foresees measures to boost the quality and efficiency of teacher in-service training:

(i)   The law abolishes the previous obligatory assessment and certification of teachers—a system vulnerable to corruption—every 5 years, coupled with in-service training provided by 25 In-Service Teacher Training (INSETT) institutes in Ukraine. Under the new law, teachers will be able to accumulate 150 hours of in-service training every 5 years. Schools will have more freedom in deciding the number of teachers, and to which in-service training courses they send their teachers. A certification system is being developed to ensure that teacher professional development efforts are recognized.

(ii)   The in-service training market will be opened to different service providers to combat corruption. An independent certification system will be created and the monopoly of INSETT institutes will be discontinued; although most of the training will still be given by the INSETT institutes as an arm of MoES.

(iii) MoES will allocate funding to the *oblasts* (administrative regions in Ukraine) and the INSETT institutes according to the number of teachers in each region.

(iv)   A national e-platform will be introduced to provide opportunities for teachers to upgrade their skills through online courses and experience exchanges or internships.

(v)   A mentoring system will be developed to ensure that teachers receive necessary support during their participation in courses or exchange visits.

The Government of Ukraine has made it a priority to find alternative, effective, relevant, and cost-effective ways of providing professional development that will reach all teachers, particularly those who are introducing new paradigms of teaching and learning. Issues that demand urgent attention for teachers are: (i) that they understand the meaning of the reforms; (ii) that they are competent in the subject matter they teach; (iii) that they know a range of methodologies; and (iv) that they approach their work with professionalism.

The language component of "Learning Together" allows for the transition from teaching Ukrainian to national minorities as a mother-tongue language to teaching it as a second language (L2) (Figure 13). Teaching Ukrainian L2 will be done through teacher training, the provision of teaching materials, and the promotion of the benefits of multilingualism and multiculturalism. To accomplish these, the language component of the project has been integrated into three main clusters: C1–Teacher Training, C2–Education Promotion, and C3–Educational Environment.

Cluster 1 (Teacher Training) activities are intended to change the methods of teaching the Ukrainian language to ethnic minority pupils and will improve the quality of teaching Ukrainian L2 to Romanian and Hungarian national minorities. It is expected that the upgraded standards, curricula, and the diversity of modern approaches and programs used for teacher professional development will be indicators of the advanced and competitive national minority language teaching system in Ukraine. It is also expected that this system will be in line with world practice: the methodology for teaching Ukrainian L2 will be developed in line with the Common European Framework of Reference for Languages.

Figure 13:   **Visualization of the Goals and Activities of the Language Component**

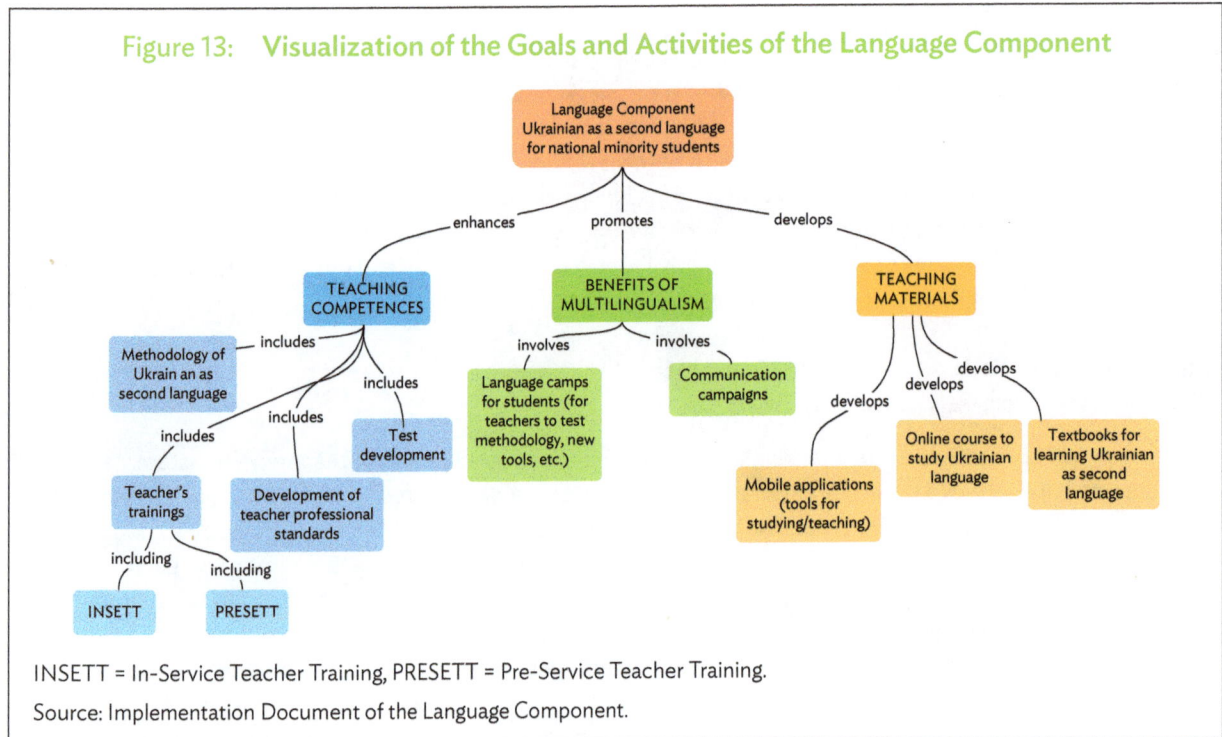

INSETT = In-Service Teacher Training, PRESETT = Pre-Service Teacher Training.

Source: Implementation Document of the Language Component.

Cluster 2 (Education Promotion) activities will increase awareness of the benefits of bilingualism and multilingualism, which is also a prerequisite for encouraging language teachers in their professional development.

Cluster 3 (Educational Environment) activities should provide a diverse set of modern teaching tools for L2 instruction (textbooks, online applications, mobile applications, etc.).

Though the knowledge-based paradigm of teaching the Ukrainian language has been applied in the country since its independence, approaches are shifting to the competency-based paradigm, effectively changing INSETT teacher training. The "Learning Together" language component is aimed at teaching the Ukrainian language and other subjects in Ukrainian for national minorities using this approach.

Some major challenges include: (i) a lack of interest in the topic, which leads to a basic lack of understanding of second languages among educators. This consequently turned the concept of the second language into a political matter; (ii) a lack of methodology for teaching Ukrainian L2; and (iii) a lack of textbooks, materials, and tools on Ukrainian for minorities.

The language component of the project aims to tackle all these challenges by providing local educators with sufficient tools to teach Ukrainian L2 to students of national minorities during basic and in-service training sessions. While benefiting from the Finnish experience in reforming the whole school education system in Ukraine, the language component also uses the Canadian experience. This was brought about due to the strong Ukrainian teacher community in Alberta, Canada, and the abundance of locally developed materials for teaching Ukrainian L2.

Results
Within less than a year (June 2019–January 2020) of implementation of the language component activities, more than 200 teachers in the Chernivtsi and Transcarpathian regions were trained to provide instruction of

Ukrainian L2. This output was achieved through the following activities: (i) Summer Academy on teaching Ukrainian L2 for teachers and teacher trainers from the Chernivtsi and Transcarpathian regions; (ii) workshops for teachers, teacher trainers, professors, and students from pedagogical universities in the Chernivtsi and Transcarpathian regions; and (iii) preparational training for teachers (trainers) in student language camps.

Summer Academy on Teaching Ukrainian L2 for Teachers and Teacher Trainers from the Chernivtsi and Transcarpathian Regions

A variety of activities for 2019 Summer Academy participants were planned and facilitated. These activities included formal presentations on a different professional development topic related to the effective teaching of Ukrainian L2. These presentations were followed up by hands-on, practical working sessions for participants. In these working sessions, teachers worked in a variety of groupings to apply their new learning to the development of lesson plans and thematic unit plans with the integration of technology. Cultural activities were organized for weekends to provide the authentic Ukrainian language and cultural events to enrich the 2019 Summer Academy experience for participants. Each cultural activity was accompanied by model lesson plans that participants could later adapt for use in their Ukrainian L2 classrooms.

Several International experts from Canada were involved based on a request by MoES. The involvement of Canadian experts was justified because there is a strong Ukrainian language teacher community in Alberta. The official languages of Canada are non-Slavic versus students having a Slavic mother tongue, and Canadians have prepared modern Ukrainian L2 material locally. All the materials are already available in Ukrainian. The material is based on the concept of student competencies. Moreover, the Ukrainian diaspora in Canada exceeds 1.2 million inhabitants versus different EU countries where the size of the Ukrainian population is considerably lower. The project would not be able to contribute anything as significant from any EU country, for instance.

According to the online feedback from Summer Academy participants, the overall quality of the Summer Academy was assessed as excellent. In general, the participants evaluated highly the expertise of the trainers, as well as the interaction between the trainers and participants. From the organizational perspective, the feedback suggested communicating with the possible participants well before the events.

Workshops for Teachers, Teacher Trainers, Professors, and Students from Pedagogical Universities in the Chernivtsi and Transcarpathian Regions

The general objective of the activity was to develop the professional skills of the participants in teaching Ukrainian L2. For this purpose, the project team set the following specific objectives: (i) to increase the insight of the participants in the fundamental approaches to teaching Ukrainian L2; (ii) to provide the participants of the Summer Academy 2019 with methodological support; and (iii) to support the formation of the professional community of teachers for experience and best practices exchange regarding teaching Ukrainian L2.

The target audience of the training program consisted of methodologists from the INSETT institute in the Transcarpathian and Chernivtsi regions, teachers of the Ukrainian language at primary school in classes with the Romanian or Hungarian languages of instruction, participants of the Summer Academy 2019, lecturers, and students of higher education institutions of pedagogical sciences. Most participants were women. Out of 170 participants, only 7 were men. They took part in all four workshops. This gender disparity is due to an overwhelming female majority of teachers in Ukraine.

In total, there were four training events in November 2019, one in the Chernivtsi region and three in the Transcarpathian region (Uzhhorod, Berehovo, and Tiachiv). In the Transcarpathian region, three workshops were held to cover a wider audience with over 100 schools offering Hungarian or Romanian languages of instruction and to lessen the logistics costs and discomfort for the participants and stakeholders.

All events had a standard program including topics such as Language Consciousness, an overview of the main approaches to teaching Ukrainian L2, and human rights.

The workshops proved to be a strong and effective tool for providing information and methodological support as well as promoting the project and communicating with the target groups. The participants showed great interest in activities as they could learn new insights into their profession and acquire new skills and approaches to interact with students. The participants also had an opportunity for informal communications with their colleagues to discuss the challenges and various difficulties they face in their everyday work, share experiences, and best practices. The human rights section was also extremely interesting and useful for the participants of the workshops. The attendees received information and ideas about human rights concepts and how they could be integrated into the education process.

An interactive approach combining lectures with interactive communications and group work proved to be more effective and interesting for the participants than conventional lectures. In future activities, local and regional mass media should be informed in advance and invited to cover the events.

It is worth continuing similar activities during project implementation, which would serve several purposes: (i) professional development of teachers and testing new methodological approaches, (ii) communication with target groups, (iii) promotion of concepts and ideas of the new Ukrainian schools, and (iv) popularization of the project activities. These measures help get closer to the target groups as communication is based on live contact and positive examples. Feedback from the workshop in Chernivtsi showed that the overall quality of the activity received "excellent" ratings from the participants. The feedback was slightly less praised in the Transcarpathian region.

Language Camps
An important component of the activities under this cluster was the language camps for students with prior in-service training for teachers (future trainers in camps). Spring Camps for 11th graders were held in the Chernivtsi and Transcarpathian regions to help school graduates prepare for the Ukrainian language external independent test. The overall goal of the summer camps was to activate and motivate students from Hungarian and Romanian communities in the Chernivtsi and Transcarpathian regions to practice their skills in the Ukrainian language. The concept of the summer camps was to achieve the output planned through creating multilingual environments in the camps by using three languages (Table 2): (i) Ukrainian as the state language and the main language of focus for instruction during the program, (ii) English as the language of international communications and the additional language of instructions, and (iii) Hungarian or Romanian as the languages of the national communities and auxiliary language for communications with students.

In general, the camps received positive feedback from students, teachers, and local communities. The programs of the camps were developed using interactive activities. However, these programs concentrated more on activities than on the pedagogical content. The number of participants of the spring and summer camps exceeded the plan. However, the camps were not able to include the more vulnerable group of children who do not speak Ukrainian at all with no motivation to visit the camp.

Lessons
Due to the ongoing decentralization of the decision-making process, some of the stakeholders did not necessarily follow the plan agreed to between the donor and MoES. This led to sudden changes affecting the smooth implementation of the activities. In such cases, the activities either were postponed, re-agreed with the stakeholder, or reorganized.

The dynamics of changes in the Ukrainian in-service teacher training system is noticeable. MoES' requests for modifications of activities of the language component are likely to happen in the future.

Table 2:   **Outputs Achieved**

Output Indicator	Planned for the Whole Project Period	Planned per Year (Summer + Spring Camps)	Fact 2019	
			Spring Camps	Summer Camps
Number of students involved	2,800	700	414	625
Chernivtsi region	n/a*	n/a	200	261
Transcarpathian region	n/a	n/a	214	364
Number of teachers trained	132	44	44	44
Chernivtsi region	66	22	22	22
Transcarpathian region	66	22	22	22

*n/a – not applicable.

Sources: Implementation Document of the Language Component; Project's Annual Report 2019.

The national curricula for teaching Ukrainian to national minorities (grades 1–9) is under preparation and hopes to be approved in 2021. Since education programs are at the heart of pedagogical activity, the condition of their timely approval becomes fundamental to almost all activities in the project's language component.

The issue of training teachers and trainers of teachers requires proper feasibility studies. This will provide the project with sufficient information to make strategic choices in designing teacher training.

The issue of the lack of companies (service providers) in Ukraine that could provide high-quality services remains significant. It may be worth expanding the selection of such providers abroad.

Sustainability

The project is based on strong ownership and leadership of the MoES, and the project implementation is closely aligned with the Venice Commission road map. However, the new Venice Commission decision provides for several recommendations that are essential for the activities of the Language Component of the project (which may affect sustainability).[3]

According to the Law on supporting the functioning of the Ukrainian language as the state language, by 2023, all the schools with minorities' languages of instruction would have to ensure that 60% of all the subjects are taught in Ukrainian. This raises concerns among the subject teachers, as MoES and state INSETT institutions are not provided with sufficient and efficient tools and techniques to make this a smooth transfer. The motivation of teachers who might be affected by the current legislation is also low due to other reasons, such as low salaries and low social status of the teaching profession, and high dependency on the school principal's decisions concerning professional development.

The language camps were effective in providing modern interactive tools for teacher professional development. The success of camps can be instructive for similar education programs in rural Ukraine and other countries. Camps could not cover the most vulnerable group of children (those with no language skills in Ukrainian) who are not motivated to visit the camp. Also, camps had a relatively new program that has yet to go to scale. With the completion of the project, the financing of such activities is likely to be complicated. It is worthwhile to reconsider the approaches of the concept of these camps, such as developing focused model language camp/summer

---

[3]   For example: "to repeal the provisions of the Law providing for a differential treatment between the languages of indigenous peoples, the languages of national minorities which are official languages of the EU and the languages of national minorities which are not official languages of the EU to the extent that the distinction between those languages is not based on an objective and reasonable justification (see European Commission, 2019, pp. 39-44, 69-82, 87, 89, 93, 94, 99-102, 110, and 111)."

school programs for Hungarian speaking students that can be replicated (multiplier effect) by all schools for national minorities, e.g., during the annual state-funded school summer camps in June.

The project will produce online training material suitable for in-service training. That material will be usable even after the completion of the project. However, the question of using electronic materials at schools after the end of the project (depreciation of equipment, network system administration, server service, etc.) remains unclear from a sustainability perspective.

Conclusions

Further field analysis of the situation in the regions is required, as regions vary considerably according to their needs and characteristics, and official information available in the central administrations is not always verified at the local level. For the same reason, the feasibility study about training sessions for teachers in mother-tongue and minority languages in the field is a particularly pressing issue. Also, there is a need to coordinate the activities of various international organizations and projects that operate in Ukraine with similar purposes of teacher development (for example, the Organization for Security and Co-operation in Europe or British Council).

Planning of activities needs to be rescheduled, as activities during holidays reduce teachers' and administrators' motivation to participate in such activities. To increase the motivation of the teachers to participate in the project's activities and training sessions, the logistics and timing of the events should be taken into account, as there are large constraints with public transportation in the remote districts in the target regions. Some of the reasons why it is important to conduct on-site training (but not online) are lack of high-speed internet connection in some of the remote settlements in the target regions, opportunity to build teachers' networks, and inspire the "agents of changes" among the professional community, and a chance to use the on-site training as a platform for testing all the tools and methods provided by the project's experts.

The project will continue with shorter training activities (half-day training sessions), and the professional development of teachers, as well as testing its newly developed methodological approaches. It will continue communications with target groups, the promotion of concepts and ideas for new Ukrainian schools, and the popularization of project activities.

The communication campaigns in targeted regions are of high importance as there is miscommunication between the Ukrainian-language and Hungarian- and Romanian-language media. Ukrainian-language media focuses on the need for national minorities to study the state language and integrate into Ukrainian society. It emphasizes the poor results of the external testing, and community speakers stress the central government's "assimilation policy" and "violation of rights to education in their native language." A strategy of positive communications should be developed that would highlight positive achievements of the project, issues uniting people, and success stories. This is crucial for teachers' motivation for professional development.

Close interaction with the national communities at all project stages—through consultation and involvement—will enable goals to be reached.

This article describes the intention to establish new practices to teach the state language to students of national minorities. With modifications, this strategy could be scaled to other linguistic environments. Human rights must be at the core of teaching L2. Students have the right to simultaneously learn in their language and gain sufficient proficiency in the state language so that they may enter further education without obstacles. Moreover, this experience would be worth studying either in countries with a similar language policy (one state language, but several local or minority languages) or in countries with a similar professional teacher development structure.

Singapore—Learning To Do, Learning To Be: A New Paradigm in Teaching and Learning

Authors: Iris Seet, Deputy Dean; Dr William Choy, Head/Pedagogic and Professional Research; and Sharon Wong, Master Mentor, ITE Academy, Institute of Technical Education (Singapore)

Background

Singapore faces similar challenges with other developed nations, such as a shrinking and aging workforce, disruptive technologies, and rapidly evolving global business trends. These trends affect the skills and jobs required by the future economy. Not surprisingly, the reskilling and upskilling of its workforce has received considerable national attention. At the same time, public-funded TVET institutions—such as the Institute of Technical Education (ITE)—are compelled to offer new ways of teaching and learning that will better prepare fresh school leavers for future work in the digital economy.

Since 2020, all full-time ITE courses of 2-year duration for fresh secondary school leavers entail a mandatory internship component of 3 to 6 months. By 2030, the Singapore Education Ministry will be ramping up workplace learning placements for each ITE student cohort from 3% to 12%. This will create a new work-study path comprising 70% on-the-job learning and 30% on-campus study.

An obvious consequence of these policy shifts is the significant reduction of curriculum time spent on campus. ITE had to rethink its conventional competency-based delivery approach: from a structured curriculum that neatly separates practical training in labs and/or workshops, and from theory classes to a more holistic model that integrates both technical knowledge and practical skills—including soft skills—in line with how learning occurs at the workplace. Seeking to foster a strong nexus between work-based learning and workplace learning, the intervention was also a response to employer survey findings that saw ITE graduates scoring well on technical competencies, but less so on soft skills that are ever more critical in the digital economy.

Intervention

Against this backdrop of change, a paradigm shift was essential. ITE teachers used to the conventional approach would have to adapt to a different way of delivering their competency-based curriculum within a shorter duration without compromising on the key learning outcomes.

As early as 2005, some ITE training facilities had begun to be designed as authentic learning spaces that mirror workplace settings that graduates will eventually find themselves in. The ensuing development of more authentic learning environments spurred a variety of pedagogic innovations that included the use of the latest technology tools by different ITE Schools. To optimize the use of such spaces and encourage more sustainable and widespread adoption of work-based teaching and learning, ITE Academy—in 2015—conceptualized its

Discipline-Specific Pedagogies (DSP) Model. This is an explicit and structured adaptation of the German and Swiss Dual Training Approach to guide teachers in exploring and developing innovative ways of delivery to suit the local contexts of various industries.

DSP provides a systematic process for the careful selection of teaching strategies that best facilitate students' acquisition of knowledge, skills, and values specific to the context, content, and practices of their chosen profession. The model draws from Shulman's idea of signature pedagogies as "the types of teaching that organize the fundamental ways in which future practitioners are educated for their new professions" (Shulman 2005). It advocates an integrated teaching and learning approach that hinges on work situations and professional and trade practices to promote the acquisition of "trade-specific DNA" in students.

At the heart of ITE's DSP are three core features:

   (i)   Development of learning situations based on industry-specific work situations to connect off-the-job learning in colleges with on-the-job training in companies.
   (ii) Contextualization of pedagogic strategies carefully chosen to align teaching and learning activities with industry-specific work practices.
   (iii) Infusion of profession-specific work attitudes, values, and dispositions along with the technical competencies in lesson planning.

The Initial Approach

DSP was featured as one of several strategic programs under ITE's 5-year Trailblazer Plan (2014–2019). Two batches of DSP pioneers comprising mainly teacher-mentors and several academic heads embarked on a 9-month study program that included a 4-week training stint at a German Teachers' Training College, as well as educational visits to German vocational colleges and companies with strong apprenticeship programs.

Upon their return, these DSP pioneers, in turn, trained fellow teachers and worked together in different trade clusters to experiment with DSP practices. In the DSP pilot completed in December 2018, the teams spent more than 750 hours training some 200 staff (13% of the teaching staff in ITE) on the new approach.

During the DSP workshops, teams of teachers collaborated to redesign lesson plans and create learning situations that require a holistic interpretation of the curriculum standard. Teachers had to draw on common work situations curated from industry visits, observations, and interviews with domain experts. The new pedagogic approach that centers on real work situations—encouraging independent inquiry, problem-solving skills, and students as co-creators—was a radical departure from carrying out teaching and learning within silo modules. Whereas the focus was once largely on "learning to do," teachers now have to attend equally to students' acquisition of generic soft skills related to the vocation, thus grooming "learning to be" future practitioners of the trade.

The academic management committees (AMC) that typically presided over specific clusters of programs across all three ITE colleges appointed members of the DSP work groups, each led by a DSP-trained pioneer.

ITE Academy headquarters is centrally responsible for the professional development of teachers and held roadshows at all three colleges to communicate the rationale and philosophy of DSP to all academic staff. It hosted bi-monthly meetings with all the work groups during various phases of the pilot to (i) review the DSPs identified by the teams, (ii) assess the perceived effectiveness of the DSPs, and (iii) address the challenges and solutions during the trial period. The trial DSP process for selected classes lasted over 2 years. At the same time, the DSP work groups presented periodic updates to their respective AMCs.

Figure 14 illustrates this change management approach.

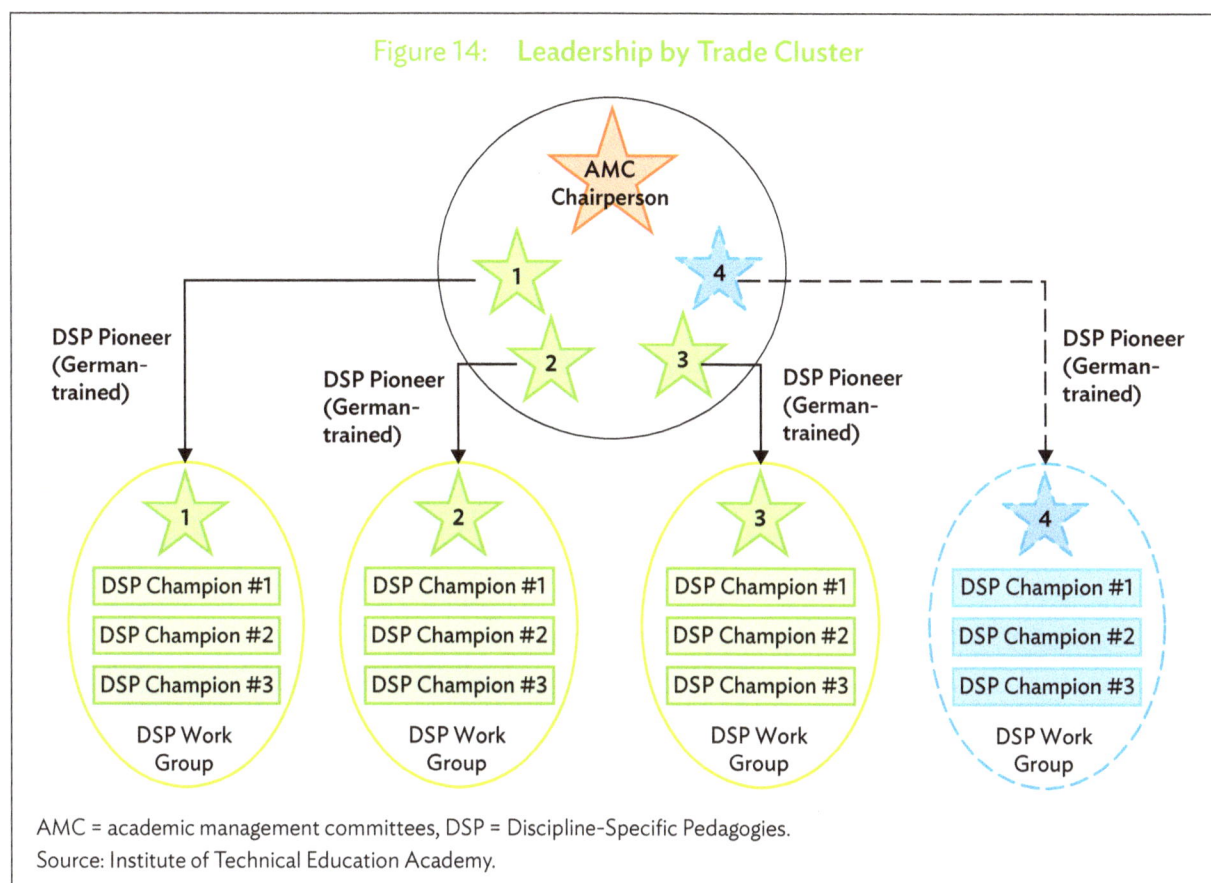

Figure 14:   **Leadership by Trade Cluster**

AMC = academic management committees, DSP = Discipline-Specific Pedagogies.
Source: Institute of Technical Education Academy.

Results of the Pilot Intervention

By March 2019, the pilot intervention saw DSP implemented in 95 classes in the three ITE colleges, involving 3,200 students. Twenty-three DSP learning packages were completed and trialed in 20 courses and subsequently refined and curated in the Pedagogy Resource System for access by all teachers (Box 1).

The post-pilot results from the teachers showed largely positive outcomes: two out of three DSP pioneers expressed plans to extend this integrated work-based teaching and learning approach to the delivery of other modules. Participants generally saw for themselves higher levels of student engagement, confidence, and motivation to perform well. Most noteworthy comments came from several teachers who admitted initial skepticism of DSP, but in due course, became convinced of its efficacy when employers gave commendable feedback on their interns' performance.

The students themselves indicated that they had a clearer understanding of the relevance of the knowledge and skills covered in the curriculum to the profession they were being prepared for. They expressed readiness for their internship, as they felt more like junior employees working alongside their "teacher-supervisor" in their learning journey on campus. A case study in School of Business Services, Institute of Technical Education College East is provided in Box 1.

Box 1: A Case Study on School of Business Services, Institute of Technical Education College East

In 2019, a team of teachers and Master Mentors ran a 1-year study to track the efficacy of scenario-based learning strategy based on core Discipline-Specific Pedagogies (DSP) principles for two classes of 73 students training to be passenger service agents in the Higher Nitec in Passenger Services course. The Master Mentors made use of surveys, lesson-with-onsite work observations, and focus group discussions with the students and their teachers to evaluate three key aspects. From April to early December 2019, the team examined (i) the level of teacher-student engagement, (ii) the teaching methods and learning activities, and (iii) the student learning, understanding, and application of skills and knowledge.

Results of the Students' Perceptions (Overall Mean Score = 3.80; Standard Deviation <0.5)

Several significant findings emerged. First, the student perception survey (100% response rate) in the figure below showed very positive results. The survey—using a four-point Likert Scale: Disagree (1), Slightly Disagree (2), Slightly Agree (3), and Agree (4)—showed a high mean score of >3.80 in all three areas. The overall standard deviation (SD) is <0.5, indicating a high level of teacher consistency for both classes concerning all three areas investigated.

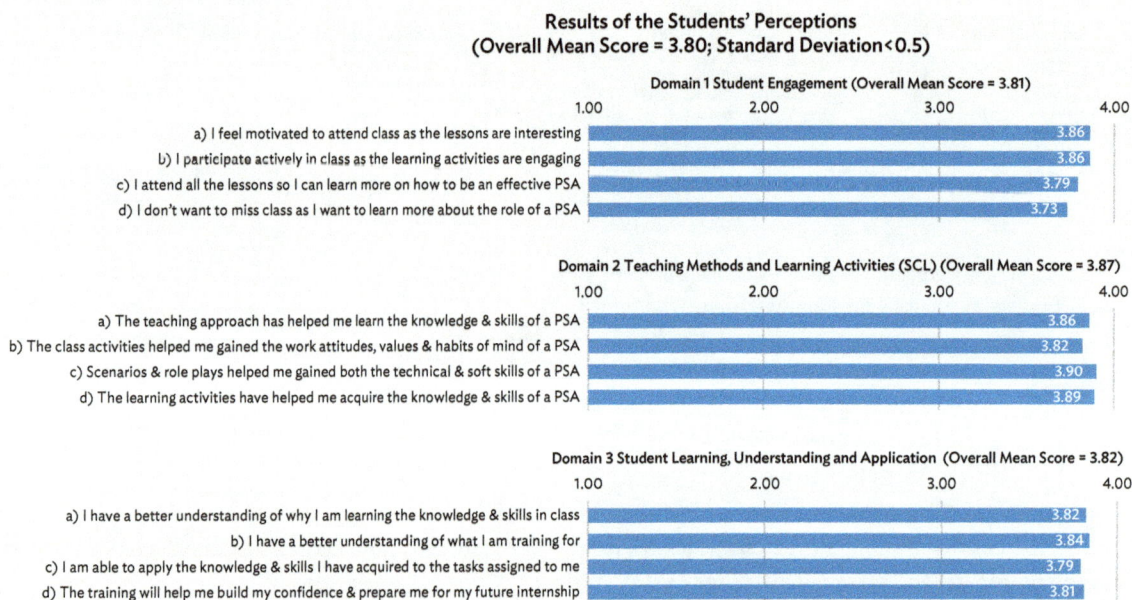

Results of the Students' Perceptions
(Overall Mean Score = 3.80; Standard Deviation<0.5)

Domain 1 Student Engagement (Overall Mean Score = 3.81)

	Score
a) I feel motivated to attend class as the lessons are interesting	3.86
b) I participate actively in class as the learning activities are engaging	3.86
c) I attend all the lessons so I can learn more on how to be an effective PSA	3.79
d) I don't want to miss class as I want to learn more about the role of a PSA	3.73

Domain 2 Teaching Methods and Learning Activities (SCL) (Overall Mean Score = 3.87)

	Score
a) The teaching approach has helped me learn the knowledge & skills of a PSA	3.86
b) The class activities helped me gained the work attitudes, values & habits of mind of a PSA	3.82
c) Scenarios & role plays helped me gained both the technical & soft skills of a PSA	3.90
d) The learning activities have helped me acquire the knowledge & skills of a PSA	3.89

Domain 3 Student Learning, Understanding and Application (Overall Mean Score = 3.82)

	Score
a) I have a better understanding of why I am learning the knowledge & skills in class	3.82
b) I have a better understanding of what I am training for	3.84
c) I am able to apply the knowledge & skills I have acquired to the tasks assigned to me	3.79
d) The training will help me build my confidence & prepare me for my future internship	3.81

PSA = passenger service agent

Considerable time spent observing the interns at the Seletar and Changi Airports showed that most were not only efficient, but also service-oriented in their work. Most noteworthy were supervisors' specific citations of some interns displaying soft skills, such as problem solving, creative thinking, and service orientation that further corroborated the work group's observations on the successful application of learning. The work supervisors proposed that the pre-attachment training could further strengthen the interns' ability to think on their feet and communicate effectively under more stressful conditions.

Through personal reflection, class debriefs and a face-to-face interview with the investigating team, the teachers affirmed their students displayed an in-depth grasp of a typical workplace situation and its performance requirements from the learning activities carefully designed following DSP principles. Interestingly, the teachers realized from their interns' feedback they had to recalibrate and step up the difficulty level of their learning activities and work scenarios.

Sources: Iris Seet, Deputy Dean; William Choy, Head/Pedagogic and Professional Research; and Sharon Wong, Master Mentor, ITE Academy, Institute of Technical Education (Singapore).

Reflections

The DSP initiative pointed to some positive learner outcomes, with all the DSP pioneers acknowledging the soundness of the approach. All agreed the experiment was successful in improving learner engagement and application of learning. Nonetheless, three key challenges were cited in its implementation. Firstly, training fellow teachers in the redesign of lessons—breaking away from the usual topical approach and creating new learning resources based on realistic workplace situations—was altogether time-consuming, complex, and challenging. Tensions persist in some areas of the curriculum—where traditional ways of teaching and learning operate— making it challenging to implement alternative practices in authentic, holistic ways. Moreover, the limited curriculum time on campus warrants a judicious balance between instructor-led and student-led inquiry.

Secondly, the post-DSP focus group discussions highlighted a necessary adjustment of the typical summative assessment of students' performance—based on theory and practical examinations for computation of an overall grade point average—to a more holistic performance-based approach that considers industry inputs as well. As assessment drives practice, further reform—possibly in the form of more integrated work-based projects—will enable both teachers and students to appreciate more deeply the connection between theory and practice.

Thirdly, the DSP approach necessitates a continual updating of teachers with the latest industry work practices to redesign the curriculum. Recognizing this imperative, respondents welcomed the provision of more support structures to be better informed and equipped to develop work situations, work-based learning activities, and assessments that are relevant and authentic to the work tasks.

Success Factors

Change process generally does not occur linearly; challenging prevailing teacher beliefs and perceptions, reforming pedagogic approaches, and—most importantly—sustaining the movement requires consistent and continual efforts that work better if the approach is not only top-down, but also bottom-up.

DSP in ITE could take off with a measure of success owing to several factors, as follows:

Timeliness of Intervention

The launch of DSP coincided with the national SkillsFuture Singapore agenda pushing for more work-study programs for both fresh school leavers and adult workers.[4] Its core principles accord well with the renewed focus on holistic skills mastery. All the key stakeholders collaborated closely with ITE Academy to make the essential policy and systemic changes to curriculum, assessment, and delivery to support the reform. The DSP pilot culminated in a comprehensive DSP training package that the ITE Academy developed and has deployed in training 320 teachers, representing 20% of ITE's faculty.

Strong Partnership with Industry

Extensive and intensive collaboration with industry partners and employers has enabled ITE to identify, design, and update its courses in time for industry changes. These strong ties established over time have helped co-create authentic curriculum and secure training placements for students. Currently, more than 3,400 employers as co-training partners offer internships and workplace learning for students. More than 200 active industries partner with schools for authentic learning and staff capability development. ITE management has also put in place support structures to facilitate industry engagement and industry attachment for faculty to maintain the currency of their domain expertise.

---

[4]   SkillsFuture Singapore: an agency within the Ministry of Education overseeing the national skills development plan for Singaporeans at different stages of their lives. Details can be found at https://www.skillsfuture.sg,

Sustaining DSP Practices via Professional Learning Circles

The DSP experiment showed that small workgroups enjoyed collaborating with peers. There was genuine sharing and open exchange of ideas, helping to shape members' knowledge, beliefs, and practices within that professional community. It also prompted teachers to think critically about their teaching practices and transform their work to a deeper level of student engagement and learning. Leveraging on the enthusiasm of those who have embraced DSP, ITE recently enhanced its Employee Innovation Framework to incentivize the formation of professional learning circles to inject fresh ideas in the areas of teaching and learning. DSP has become both a top-down and ground-up approach. At the grassroots level, a rising number of professional learning circles formed voluntarily by teachers have begun action research in DSP, including those entailing the use of most recent technologies in smart manufacturing hubs and mixed reality labs for their respective courses.

Conclusion

Discipline-Specific Pedagogies—as adapted and practiced in ITE's context—have received strong management support and funding. ITE aims to enhance teachers' pedagogic skills and foster continual inquiry into innovative strategies that will better prepare students for the future of work, even as Industry 4.0 further evolves in the working world.

Two new programs, "Foster Work Readiness through Work Situation Curricular Approach" and "Expand Work-Study Programmes with Industry" in ITE's new Strategic Plan (2020–2024), will ensure the continuing evolution of this pedagogic reform movement. As ITE Academy trains more teachers to deliver new Work-Study Diploma programs over the next few years, it plans to undertake a more detailed assessment of the efficacy of DSP as data from a wider spread of teachers and students become available.

Viet Nam—Industry-Led Teacher Training on Industry 4.0 Requirements for Vocational Education and Training

Author: Bach Hung Truong, team leader (Supporting High-Quality TVET Institutes, GIZ Programme Reform of TVET, Viet Nam).

Background

With a population of 95 million and a labor force of over 55 million (Government of Viet Nam, General Statistics Office [GSO] 2018), Viet Nam considers improving the quality of its human resources a priority requirement for the country's sustainable development. As of 2018, only 21.9% (about 12 million persons) of the Vietnamese workforce qualified as trained workers, having completed a professional or vocational training of 3 months or above (GSO 2018). The shortage of skilled workers is hindering the country's efforts to move up the global value chain and one that is perceived by enterprises as a bigger obstacle to business expansion than wage levels, payroll taxes, or employment protection legislation (World Bank 2013).

The vocational education and training (VET) system in Viet Nam expanded significantly to meet the demands of the business sector, reaching about 2.2 million new enrollments in 2017. The three levels of VET account for (i) 75.5% (1.6 million persons) for elementary programs (3–12 months of training), (ii) 14.0% (310,000 persons) for intermediate programs (1–2 years of training), and (iii) 10.5% (230,400 persons) for college programs (2–3 years of training and new enrollments) (DVET 2017). However, while learners' return on investment proved to be significant at the elementary VET level, the value added of an intermediate VET or a VET college degree is almost negligible.

Labor market data show that workers with an elementary VET degree earn an average monthly wage of D6.6 million, about 1.3 times higher than that of their unskilled counterparts (D5 million).[5] However, the income gain does not continue with more advanced levels of qualifications. Intermediate-level workers earn only D5.8 million, and college VET degree workers earn only D6.3 million; less than those with elementary VET training, although more than unskilled workers (GSO 2018). At the same time, college-level graduates account for 8.3% of the unemployed population, compared with 6.3% for intermediate-level graduates, 2.2% for elementary-level graduates, and 2.4% for untrained workers (GSO 2018).

The low competitiveness and limited value of VET qualifications—especially at higher VET levels on the labor market—are largely attributable to a severe mismatch between VET programs and industry standards (International Labour Organzation [ILO] 2016). In response, cooperation with business has been embedded more prominently in the policy and legal framework regulating VET activities in Viet Nam. Standards for VET quality accreditation have embraced industry linkages as a key element (Ministry of Labour, Invalids, and Social Affiars 2017). The 2019 Labour Code also provided a tripartite mechanism for the cooperative training model and other forms of business sector involvement in VET to be operational and regulated by law (National Assembly 2019). However, the gap between sound policies and good practice remains significant, as only less than 10% of enterprises nationwide are reported to have cooperation ties with VET institutes (DVET 2018).

VET teacher's training and development

The ongoing efforts to strengthen industry linkages in VET are directed at the creation of internship and job placements for VET students (DVET 2018). Meanwhile, the quality of VET teachers also suffers heavily from the lack of specific mechanisms to ensure proper levels of industry experience and exposure.

The 2014 VET law and subsequent regulations on VET teachers defined three main sets of competency requirements for VET teachers, including (i) occupational, (ii) pedagogical, and (iii) computer literacy (MOLISA 2013).

Teachers are required to have a degree from at least an intermediate-level training program, or a certificate of occupational skills in relevant professional fields to teach at the elementary VET level. At the intermediate and college levels, the requirements for VET teachers depend on whether they teach theoretical or practical subjects only, or both. For theoretical teachers, the required qualifications include a bachelor's degree from a relevant university program. For practical teachers, the required qualifications include either a college-level degree or a certificate of occupational skills in relevant professional fields. For teachers teaching both theoretical and practical subjects, the requirements of both strands must be fulfilled.

Besides meeting occupational requirements, VET teachers must also possess pedagogical and computer literacy certificates applicable to the level of VET that they teach.

Since the qualifications requirements for VET teachers do not include any compulsory level of industry experience, many enter the profession with a purely academic background, equipped only with a degree from universities, colleges, or secondary schools. Subsequently, industry experience continues to be overlooked in in-service training and capacity development. The 2014 VET law stipulates that VET teachers "have the responsibility and be allowed by their managing VET institutes to make time for internships in enterprises to update and improve practical skills and approach new technology as regulated" (National Assembly 2014). It was not until 2017 that specific regulations were issued to require a minimum of 4 weeks of company-based internship annually for VET teachers at the college and intermediate levels, and 1 week for VET teachers at the elementary level (DVET 2018).

---

[5] $1 = D23,300.

Although limited, data indicate that cooperative activities between business and VET institutes to keep VET teachers current with industry developments are rare. A study conducted jointly by the National Institute of Vocational Education and Training and the Vietnam Chamber of Commerce and Industry showed that out of the 79 surveyed enterprises, only about 36% were ready to receive VET teachers for internships (DVET 2018). Data from the Department of Employment under the Ministry of Labour–Invalids and Social Affairs also confirmed that the most common forms of cooperation between enterprises and VET institutes do not include activities centered around VET teachers (DVET 2019). A 2017 survey of VET teachers from 53 out of 63 Vietnamese provinces shows that only 16.83% have an occupational skills certificate (DVET 2018).

Industry-Led Capacity Development on Industry 4.0 for Teachers at LILAMA 2
Located in Dong Nai—one of the country's economically fastest-growing provinces (Viet Nam Chamber of Commerce and Industry–United States Agency for International Development [VCCI-USAID] 2019) and home to large industrial zones—LILAMA 2 International Technology College enrolls an average of 1,300 students annually to cater for human resources needs from businesses in the southeastern region of Viet Nam. The college's flagship programs are in the fields of mechanical engineering, mechatronics, electronics, and construction.[6] As one of the country's few fully autonomous vocational education and training (VET) colleges, LILAMA 2 has a keen interest in improving the quality of its training programs to increase enrollment and expand its other businesses. It makes efforts to build and strengthen cooperation ties with business to develop occupational descriptions, establish cooperative training programs, and ensure in-company training and job placements for its students.

In 2014, LILAMA 2 became a key partner of the Vietnamese-German program "Reform of TVET in Vietnam," implemented jointly by the Deutsche Gesellschaft für Internationale Zusammenarbeit (GIZ) and Viet Nam's Directorate of Vocational Education and Training on behalf of the Federal Ministry of Economic Cooperation and Development. Aimed at bringing about quality reform for the Vietnamese VET system in the direction of greater demand-orientation and skills development for a greener economy, the program sets up models for good practices at key VET institutes and feeds back successful experiences to the country's VET system. At LILAMA 2, the objective is to develop and pilot the delivery of college-level training programs oriented on German standards for four occupations: metal cutting, construction mechanics, industrial electronics, and mechatronics. The business sector was involved in every step of the process to ensure that graduates achieve quality skills that are relevant to the labor market.

Acknowledging that the quality of VET teachers has a direct and decisive impact on students' skills development, a training package for teachers was built into the program. The expected outcome was to bring the competency level of the selected teachers up to the standards applied for skilled workers in Germany. Since 2016, 18 key teachers in Metal Cutting and Mechatronics completed a series of intensive further training in Viet Nam and Germany and were assessed by examiners from the German Chambers of Skills Crafts (Handwerkskammer). Achieving success rates ranging from 65% to 93%, LILAMA 2 teachers proved that they have the required competencies to provide not only high-quality initial training for VET students, but also further training for peer VET teachers in Viet Nam.

Industry 4.0 competencies were determined as an essential requirement to revise the training program for mechatronics from job analysis exercises conducted. However, while prospective employers insisted that Industry 4.0 be part of the new training program, LILAMA 2 teachers found themselves in need of substantial capacity building before they can confidently teach. Moreover, to keep abreast of fast-changing developments generated by Industry 4.0, regular industry exposure—as opposed to one-off training arrangements—is required. A long-term partnership with industry would, therefore, be instrumental to ensure the sustainability of skills training for both teachers and students. Bosch-Rexroth was identified as a potential partner because of the company's long history of recruiting students from LILAMA 2 and its leading Internet of Things technologies.

---

[6]   VCCI-USAID. 2019. The Vietnam Provincial Competitiveness Index 2018.

In 2018, the program "Reform of TVET in Vietnam" received approval to implement a development partnership financed jointly by the BMZ and Bosch-Rexroth. The overall objective of the project is to enhance the supply of skilled workers meeting the requirements of Industry 4.0 in Viet Nam. The main project outcomes include (i) trained VET teachers and in-company trainers to act as multipliers on Industry 4.0 requirements; (ii) enhanced capacity in Industry 4.0 for a large scale of VET teachers and in-company trainers through training delivered by multipliers; and (iii) Integration of Industry 4.0 requirements in existing VET training programs.

Results

LILAMA 2, Bosch-Rexroth, DVET, and the program "Reform of TVET in Vietnam" made official their joint commitment in August 2018. An Industry 4.0 lab was inaugurated the following month on LILAMA 2's campus, featuring training equipment in drive and control technology, technical manuals, training software, and eLearning devices from Bosch-Rexroth. The inauguration of the lab was an opportunity for representatives from the government, industry, civil society, TVET institutes, and international organizations to come together and share their views in a conference on "How Industry 4.0 is shaping the future of VET."

Inauguration of the Industry 4.0 Lab on the LILAMA 2 campus. Fully equipped with Bosch-Rexroth technology, the lab has been used for the training of VET teachers and in-company trainers since 2019 (photo from GIZ Reform of TVET in Vietnam Program, 2018).

Considering inputs generated from the inaugural conference, an enterprise survey was conducted jointly by LILAMA 2 and Bosch-Rexroth to understand different levels of Industry 4.0 skills requirements for workers in the fields of electronics and mechatronics. Findings from the survey were used to inform the proposal on the Integration of Industry 4.0 requirements into existing VET training programs. The proposal was presented in a consultation workshop to collect feedback from industry and VET practitioners before further steps were taken.

In October 2019, a 4-day training of the first unit of the training for the trainers' module was delivered by Bosch-Rexroth's in-company trainers and German experts from the program "Reform of TVET in Vietnam." The module is intended to have a strong focus on hands-on, technical exercises to demonstrate the requirements of Industry 4.0 skills in technicians' tasks and to help participants become familiar with new technology such as cyber-physical systems. Fifteen VET teachers and in-company trainers took part in the training.

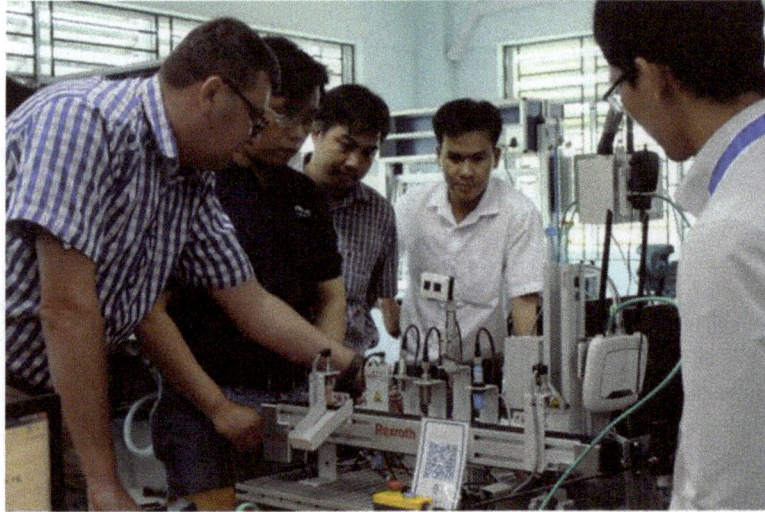

The training course "Train the Trainers with Industry 4.0" was delivered jointly by Bosch-Rexroth in-company trainers and German experts from the "Reform of TVET in Vietnam" program (photo from GIZ program Reform of TVET in Vietnam Program, 2019).

After the rollout of the Bosch-Rexroth's training module, selected participants were also given the opportunity to attend the "Put Industry 4.0 into competencies" training organized by the Regional Cooperation Programme to improve the quality and labor market orientation of technical and vocational education and training in collaboration with the South East Asian Ministers of Education Organisation, Regional Centre for Vocational and Technical Education and Training in Thailand. Designed and delivered by experts from the Association of Southeast Asian Nation countries, the training focused on capacity development for VET teachers in the context of Industry 4.0. Participants explored three modules: (i) Innovative Teaching and Learning for Industrial Changes due to Industry 4.0; (ii) Professional Development Training for TVET Teachers in Industry 4.0; and (iii) Curriculum Design for Industry 4.0 Work Process. Experience-sharing between ASEAN countries, updates on good practices in the region, and company visits were also part of the training program. Upon their return, participants disseminated the training to another 24 VET teachers from 13 VET institutes in Viet Nam.

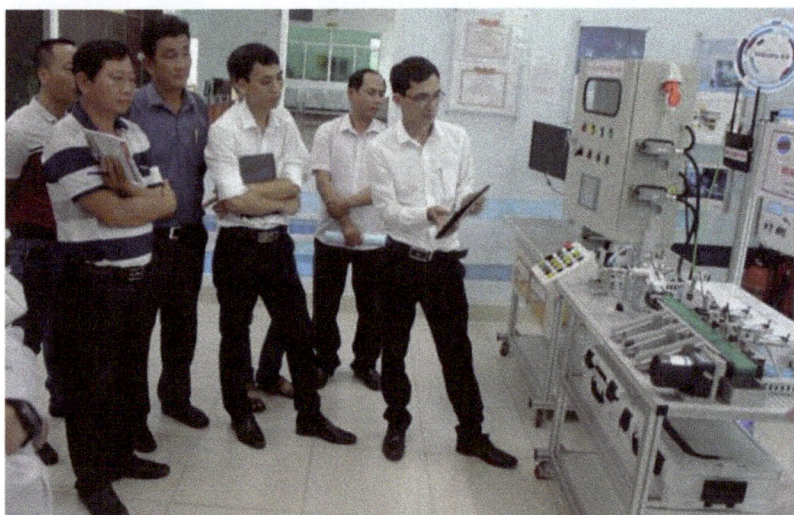

LILAMA 2 teacher/multiplier delivering Modules 2 and 3 of the "Professional Development Training for TVET Teachers in I.4.0" (photo from GIZ program "Reform of TVET in Vietnam," 2020).

By end of 2020, LILAMA 2 will offer a full package of VET teachers' in-service training on Industry 4.0. The package includes two major components: (i) a practice-oriented module aimed at enhancing Industry 4.0 skills for VET teachers and in-company trainers in mechatronics and electrotechnics, and (ii) a set of three modules to build capacity for VET teachers to effectively respond to new Industry 4.0 requirements.

As of early 2020, seven VET institutes and two enterprises in Viet Nam have expressed their interest in attending the training package, either in full or in selected units of content.

Lessons

In the context of fast changing technology, training for VET teachers—not unlike training for VET graduates—needs to be aligned with and driven by industry demand. Bosch-Rexroth's leading role in the Industry 4.0 training-of-trainers program proves instrumental in generating interest from VET practitioners and in-company trainers. Moreover, despite being among Viet Nam's leading VET institutes, it would be challenging for LILAMA 2 to secure proper equipment for training, qualified trainers, and training content had it not been for the partnership with Bosch-Rexroth.

The value proposition that underpins the partnership with Bosch-Rexroth is a strong one that specifies clear win-win benefits for involving parties from the start. Without reasonable benefits, it would be difficult for private sector partners to cooperate with VET institutes.

The involvement of Bosch-Rexroth's in-company trainers helped showcase the role and importance of in-company trainers in enterprise-based training. As the Vietnamese VET system is heavily school-based, the formation of in-company trainers is an area of great potential for future development. Quite a few companies and VET institutes who experienced the initial Industry 4.0 training subsequently expressed their interest in the training for in-company trainers delivered jointly by Bosch-Rexroth and LILAMA 2.

Challenges

Effective human resources management proved to be a challenge for LILAMA 2 during the process, as master trainers selected among key teachers often have a heavy workload and cannot easily accommodate additional tasks.

As technical materials, and many of the training opportunities are available in English, the selection of participants with sufficient English proficiency was another challenge faced by the intervention.

Ethiopia—Teachers are Changemakers: Toward Inclusive Education in Technical and Vocational Education

Authors: Maija Mäkinen; PhD, principal lecturer (JAMK University of Applied Sciences, Finland) and Yekunoamlak Alemu; PhD, assistant professor of HRD/TVET and Educational Leadership (Addis Ababa University, Ethiopia)

Background

This article examines how an international project can have an impact on the educational development of the partner country, with the Teacher Educators in Higher Education as Catalysts for Inclusive Practices (TECIP) project as an example. This is a collaborative project aimed at the promotion of inclusive education in TVET teacher education in Ethiopia. The Ministry for Foreign Affairs of Finland has supported Ethiopia in the education sector development for years, focusing on inclusive education. The TECIP project is the continuation of the cooperation, expanding to a new education sector. The project is considered a developmental agent that can have an impact on attitudes, skills, and knowledge of actors which, in turn, can lead to sustainable changes in inclusive practices in TVET. The project's target groups were TVET teacher trainers, TVET administration, and

TVET teachers at the grassroots level at TVET colleges. The project's target groups were TVET teacher trainers, TVET administration, and TVET teachers at the grassroots level at vocational colleges (JAMK 2020).

The World Report on Disability (World Bank and World Health Organization 2011) estimated that there were 15 million people with disabilities in Ethiopia, representing 17.6% of the total population at the time. Similarly, 95% of people with disabilities in Ethiopia live in poverty (Malle 2017), most of them in rural areas, where basic services are limited and the chances of accessing rehabilitative or support services are remote. Only 3% of Ethiopia's estimated 2.4 million–4.8 million children with disabilities go to school. Only 0.5% of them continue to technical and vocational education. This is due to stigma among parents and educators, inaccessibility, rigid teaching practices, poorly trained teachers, and the lack of adapted learning resources (Malle 2017). The Government of Ethiopia has taken legislative and policy steps that indicate a commitment to advancing the rights of persons with disabilities. At present, there is a favorable policy environment for developing post-secondary TVET toward inclusion. Still, concrete actions are needed. Because teachers have a key role in enacting reforms, the development of TVET teacher education is the prime objective for ensuring people with special education needs and disabilities get access to and participate in TVET education (Mäkinen et al. 2019).

Before the beginning of the TECIP-project, the share of students with special education needs and disabilities in TVET colleges was quite low. Staff for inclusive education was lacking (Malle 2017), and attitudinal barriers existed. There was also a need for a suitable curriculum, adaptive educational materials, and facilities in all teacher education levels (Malle 2017).

The project started by reevaluating TVET teacher education for inclusion at the beginning of September 2017. The key persons in teacher education of the Federal TVET Institute (FTI) and Addis Ababa University (AAU) were invited to Finland to attend a workshop to examine the situation and compare it to the planning of the project. Although FTI was nominated as the main beneficiary, AAU was the leading university in inclusive education in Ethiopia and was chosen as a partner. To specify the situation at the beginning of the project in 2017, baseline information was collected via qualitative and more structured questionnaires from 111 TVET administrators and 75 TVET teacher trainers in November 2017 (Mäkinen et al. 2019).

Major organizational changes simultaneously provide a possibility for a new way of thinking. These changes may act like cornerstones, which help workers to look forward to the future (Kajamaa 2015). Heikkilä and Seppänen (2014) speak of transformative agency, where the agency is regarded as the subject's capacity to take purposeful action to change their work.

Ethiopian and Finnish project actors in the planning phase in 2017
(photo by TECIP project).

Goals of the TECIP project

The TECIP was a capacity-building project (2017–2019) between JAMK University of Applied Sciences, Finland; the FTI, Ethiopia; AAU, Ethiopia; and the University of Jyväskylä, Finland. The mission of the TECIP project was to equip the TVET teacher training providers at the national, regional, and local levels with the necessary skills and knowledge on inclusive practices to support national development efforts toward inclusive TVET education in Ethiopia. As an outcome of the project, the TVET teacher training institute, FTI, develops its education structures to include TVET and has curricula on inclusive education and related modules for pre- and in-service TVET teacher programs. As the modules developed during the project are part of the curricula, the results sustain and reach a new generation of teachers. Additionally, a new in-service training model is being developed for FTI and piloted for future use. The project scope involves all regions of Ethiopia via the in-service training model (JAMK 2020).

Contribution of the Project on the Educational Development

In a country like Ethiopia—where administration plays an important role—it is essential to combine sustainable educational and administrative development and ensure their cooperation toward goals. To mobilize the development toward inclusion in TVET colleges, awareness-raising events were organized for TVET administration and heads of TVET colleges in five cities at the beginning of the project in 2017. The goal was to collect baseline information regarding awareness of inclusion and related issues from the key administrative stakeholders, meaning that TVET administrators set up a development process. These events recruited more than 100 participants, and 111 completed questionnaires concerning their opinions on inclusive education.

While there was concern regarding the implementation of inclusion, several respondents reported having good personal and/or organizational experiences regarding efforts to teach people with disabilities. Many good solutions had already been implemented at various levels—albeit not widely—and experience had been gained in organizing support and adjusting for students with disabilities. When respondents were asked to list the major challenges to implementing inclusion, their responses included facilities, materials and equipment, skilled workforce, curriculum, and attitudes. The contribution of the Ethiopian TVET administration—the Federal TVET Agency—was important. The agency directed TVET heads to prepare Special Needs Action Plans for their regions and TVET Colleges which were under inspection during the project (Mäkinen et al. 2019).

The other pedagogical intervention was started with an awareness raising day for the whole staff of FTI in November 2017. A questionnaire was created and delivered to 75 teacher trainers at FTI to determine the attitudinal level and readiness for change concerning their knowledge, practices, and future interests regarding inclusion. Based on the findings, a 5-week training was planned for 17 teachers of FTI. They represented different departments because the goal was to establish a special needs education coordinator system for FTI. The content of the inclusion training was divided into three sections:

(i) **Basics in inclusion in Ethiopia.** To familiarize oneself with the concept of inclusion and situation in Ethiopia; to elaborate own experiences, skills, knowledge, and future needs; to start discussions on how to do research-based developmental work in teacher training. The teaching content: The state of education of persons with disabilities in Ethiopia, The concept of inclusion, Learning support: student's viewpoint, The profile of inclusive teacher, Curriculum issues and inclusive education, and How to create inclusive teacher education and promote inclusive teaching.

(ii) **Disability perspectives in Ethiopia.** Diversity of students with disabilities in TVET and how to support students' learning and participation with inclusive teaching methods; to get more information on the education needs of students with learning difficulties, especially students with hearing and visual impairment; to get to know how to support learning, accessing, and participating of students with special education needs in TVET; to embrace the teaching skills to work with students with special education needs; and to find out how to work as an inclusive teacher trainer.

(iii)   **Inclusive education from an international context.** To find out and elaborate good inclusive practices for TVET and teacher education, to get familiar with the Finnish TVET system, and to get to know support for employment in Finland.

Most of the trainers were Ethiopian—professionals from AAU and disability organizations—to ensure the right cultural context. The Finnish professionals provided a student-centered, activating teaching methodology. Trainees received personal learning plans and two of them got a 3-month scholarship to Finland to prepare for doctorate degrees.

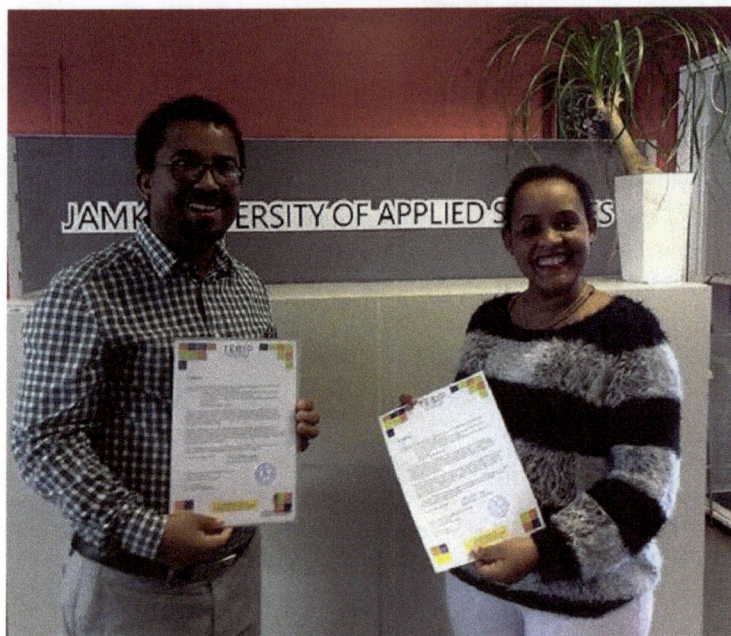

Successful training opportunity. Temesgen Tadele (left) and Tiegist Bayleyegn (right) after completing the study visit to Finland in 2019 (photo by TECIP project).

The training was synchronized with the development of a learning module on inclusion for FTI´s pre- and in-service training. The learning material was developed in close collaboration with Ethiopian persons with disabilities, AAU, and FTI teacher trainers. It was modified into the syllabus form used in FTI and adopted as part of the TVET teacher training curriculum by the Educational Senate of FTI (JAMK 2020). The syllabus of the module Introduction to Inclusive Education is provided in Box 2.

Box 2:   Syllabus Module—Introduction to Inclusive Education

Course Description

Students will be introduced to the historical development, philosophy, fundamental knowledge on inclusive education, and the rational for the paradigm shift toward inclusive education. The implications of inclusive education on students' psychosocial wellbeing, moral development, and in the promotion of social justice, human rights, as well as its cost-effectiveness will be thoroughly examined.

Students will also be exposed to the principles and dynamics of inclusive education practices in TVET focusing on students with disability. Students will be familiarized with contemporary international and national issues of inclusive education. Finally, deliberations and reflections will be made on strategies of how to effectively implement inclusive education in TVET institutions in the country.

Box 2   *continued*

Course outline

1. Historical development and trends in the education of persons with disabilities
    1.1   Special Education, Special Needs Education or Inclusive Education
          1.1.1   Subject matter (concepts and definitions)
          1.1.2   Conceptualizing disability (in particular, the way that medical and social models have influenced and shaped current thinking)
    1.2   Rational for the paradigm shift toward inclusive education

2. Implications of inclusive education on psychosocial development, social justice, and cost-effectiveness
    2.1   Inclusive education versus psychosocial development
          2.1.1   Psychological and socio-emotional
          2.1.2   Life skills (collaborative, interpersonal communication skills, etc.)
          2.1.3   Moral and ethical development
          2.1.4   Attitudinal issues
    2.2   Inclusive education versus social justice and cost-effectiveness
          2.2.1   Inclusive education, and human rights, moral and ethical issues
          2.2.2   Inclusive education and cost-effectiveness

3. Inclusive Education in TVET
    3.1   Learning characteristics of student with special needs
    3.2   Curriculum (comprehensive and all-embracing)
    3.3   Teaching and instruction (learners' center, collaborative and outcome-based)
    3.4   Technology support (software, digital and assistive technology, etc.)
    3.5   Assessment (flexible, continuous, and multiple)

4. Contemporary issues on inclusive education
    4.1   International perspectives
          4.1.1   When and where to start?
          4.1.2   Inclusive service environment (universal design)
    4.2   National perspectives
          4.2.1   Policy and strategies of inclusive education
          4.2.2   Practices of inclusive education

5. Reflection on creating an inclusive environment in TVET

(Discussion and reflection on prioritizing areas of intervention)

    5.1   Inclusive or zero rejection policy formulation (admission, placement, follow-up, graduation tracking)
    5.2   Creating an enabling environment for all students (barrier free social and physical environment)
    5.3   Establishment of inclusive education support center (back-up support for support for students, teachers, and others in need by organizing awareness raising program on inclusive education, short-term refreshment training programs on inclusive for the staff, undertaking institute based-action research to improve the quality of the inclusive education, etc.)

Developing inclusive institute culture (extra-curricular activities, multicultural programs, etc.)

TVET = technical and vocational education and training.
Source: Teacher Educators in Higher Education as Catalysts for Inclusive Practices project.

One important pedagogical intervention was to organize two rounds of training for teachers from TVET colleges from all around the country (TOT training). To ensure the sustainability of the developmental results, 100 TVET teachers at the grassroots level were offered training for 2 weeks in two rounds (February 2018 and August 2018). The first training had 75 participants, and the second training had 90 participants, with the ongoing unrest in some regions hindering the participation of all invitees. Among the trainees only 13.3% were females, implying a low level of female participation in the TVET system (Mäkinen et al. 2019).

A total of 73.3% of teachers in TVET colleges had their first degree below the minimum policy standard used in specialized institutes like TVET colleges. The participants from 54 TVET colleges represented 31 areas of specialization, with Building Construction (18.7%), ICT (9.3%), Special Needs (6.7%), and Manufacturing (6.7%) being among the leading areas. Conversely, 56% of the participants indicated that students with disabilities did not exist in their classrooms. Sixty percent of the respondents confirmed that they were not aware of inclusion before the training. About 55% of the participants were interested in inclusion. Most of the participants contended that the training was very good and transparent. They also stressed that the training environment was favorable and inclusive. On top of these benefits, the same group of respondents appreciated student-centered, participatory methodology and diverse styles of learning, learning by doing, and group-based exercises in the training. Theoretical and practical training was relevant and enabled participants to know national and international policies and practices to identify their challenges on inclusive development in TVET colleges (Mäkinen et al. 2019).

The participants learned how to create social awareness and manage classroom practices. According to the feedback, the trainees stressed the importance of actively participating in the teaching, as they had the opportunity to explore the student-centered approach as a student. They went through a new experience, which gave them tools to manage classroom practices. The training was cumulative: every trainee planned to share experiences from the training with colleagues and apply them in their TVET colleges.

Similarly, the participants stated minimal follow-up and supervision by the federal and regional TVET authorities as a big challenge as well as the recruitment of students with disabilities in TVET colleges. Lack of resources, career structure, and incentive mechanisms for those TVET teachers who work for inclusion in TVET colleges were also stated as problems. An attitude problem exists among some TVET teachers about making TVET inclusive. There is a need for further cooperation and commitment among high schools, local authorities, and TVET authorities to create awareness and recruit students with disabilities in TVET colleges (Mäkinen et al. 2019).

The success of both pieces of training was based on several factors, high motivation of trainees being one of them. Between the two training rounds, all trainees had to prepare an action plan to be implemented in their college. This encouraged them to learn. An "inclusive pedagogy" was introduced, consisting of (i) activating methods, (ii) doing together, (iii) encouraging for participation and sharing, (iv) reflection, and (v) valuing diversity. The Ethiopian trainers included "Disability Organizations" to ensure Ethiopian relevance.

One essential part of the pedagogical intervention was to ensure progress after the training. Monitoring visits were made twice to 10 TVET colleges representing different regions of Ethiopia. Quantitative as well as qualitative methods were used in the monitoring: Participant observation, questionnaires, checklists, and face-to-face open discussions with TVET teachers, who participated in the training. Apart from helping the teachers to fill in the questionnaires, the facilitators were able to interview the TVET teachers, to provide transparent and in-depth information on the impact of the training. Feedback sessions were organized for leaders of the TVET colleges, regional TVET agencies, the Federal TVET Agency, and the Federal TVET Institute. Except for some positive developments (such as the provision of incentives for students with disabilities, mainstreaming inclusive practices, or conducting needs assessment at the surrounding high schools), awareness-raising attempts were weak in the monitored TVET colleges. This is partly due to the low motivation of TVET teachers, lack of expertise in special needs education, and inadequate support from leaders. The TVET colleges also need to improve the physical accessibility (roads, buildings, ramps, toilets) and strengthen resource centers (Mäkinen et al. 2019).

In summary, although the training is aimed at improving the situation of students with disabilities, its level of implementation is still at an early stage. There is a need for continuing the support to TVET colleges and scale-up their inclusive practices (Mäkinen et al. 2019).

Training for teachers. Technical and vocational education and training teachers during a training session in 2018 (photo from the TECIP project).

The TECIP project formulated an in-service model for FTI's use in the future. The inclusive module has been adopted into the pre-service training of TVET teachers at FTI. Additionally, the project process was formed into an in-service training model for FTI. The specialized group of 17 teacher trainers from FTI conducted 2 weeks of training for 620 teacher education graduates in September 2019 focusing the teaching material on inclusion. One important milestone has been reached: The role of 17 TVET teacher trainers has been established as "special needs education coordinators." The 17 teacher trainers will conduct inclusive training for all TVET teacher education students annually. They have been also nominated to train in in-service training such as for TVET teachers or managers from the field.

TVET Teacher Trainers and Teachers as Change Agents

In the TECIP project, change was initiated by combining TVET administration with developmental steps in teacher education. The role of every teacher is important in inclusive education. Therefore, the TECIP project concentrated on improving the skills and knowledge of TVET teacher educators and TVET teachers across the country. Competence development was regarded as positive. The project seemed to increase the empowerment and awareness of trainees. The respondents referred to "an alternative approach in teaching," which was new for them. The dialogue increased the participants' possibilities to adopt new knowledge and build networks. The self-evaluation technique enhanced new learning, as did systematic planning. No educational development on the national level would have been promoted without synchronized cooperation with the TVET administration (Mäkinen et al. 2019).

Positive feedback was huge. The trainees have taken many purposeful, goal-oriented actions toward inclusion. Obstacles that were interpreted as insurmountable at the beginning of the project were regarded as merely challenging in the end, and no clear resistance to the development was visible. There was a lot of envisioning the future: great hope that challenges in the development of inclusive education will be tackled through collaboration. To enhance transformative agency, project actors need to have a feeling of empowerment. Native trainers should be prioritized, and European partners should ensure sufficient information on the social context, political, and economic situation, and effects of globalization. This ensures that global knowledge can be successfully applied on a local level. The example of the TECIP project showed that an international project can initiate a change in attitudes, knowledge, and skills of actors. However, to get sustainable changes in inclusive

TVET, there is a long way to go with TVET administration, TVET teacher education, and TVET Colleges joining hands (Mäkinen et al. 2019).

Discussion

The role of TVET education is important in training competent, motivated, and innovative professionals who can contribute to poverty reduction and social and economic development. The Ethiopian Ministry of Education has drafted a plan—Education Development Roadmap (2018–30)—including responsibilities for the TVET education sector to support equitability: guidelines for skill training to be inclusive in urban and rural communities, plans for supporting academically successful students as well as dropouts in general education, promotion of gender parity as well as ensuring access to TVET for people with special needs (Tirussew et al. 2018). Since teachers are changemakers in society, the road map calls for modernization of teacher education in Ethiopia: to prepare and launch a comprehensive teacher preparation and development policy that covers key issues related to recruitment, selection, in-service training, certification, and continuous professional development of teachers. The new education road map pays attention to the development of inclusive education and the quality of teacher education. Similarly, the goal of the TECIP project was to increase access to and participation in TVET education for people with special education needs and disabilities. The Federal TVET Institute can continue the development and work as a flagship for inclusive TVET teacher education in Ethiopia (Mäkinen et al. 2019).

4 Cases in Higher Education

Bangladesh—Centers of Excellence in Teaching and Learning

Author: Jon Harle, Director of Programs, International Network for Advancing Science and Policy (INASP) (United Kingdom)

Introduction

Bangladesh has identified a need to significantly increase the quality of teaching and learning in its universities, following significant expansion in the last decade (Parvin undated). Employers reportedly express frustration with the quality of graduates, and the inability of the higher education system to support a growing economy. Teaching is often based on rote-learning with little opportunity to develop higher-order cognitive and critical thinking skills (Rahman et al. 2019). University infrastructure or building construction programs have dominated much of the investment in the sector (Bin Tariq 2020) whereas support to academic faculty to improve teaching or improve curricula has been limited.

The need to improve pedagogical practices and strengthen quality assurance mechanisms was recognized in the Ministry of Education's 2010 national education policy and the Planning Commission's seventh Five-Year Plan (Raqib 2019). Between 2009 and 2018, the World Bank allocated $216 million through the Higher Education Quality Enhancement Project (HEQEP), working with the government to invest in ICT infrastructure and systems, a digital library program, a central quality assurance unit, and institutional management information systems, research funds and PhD scholarships (World Bank 2019). However, there was little obvious focus on pedagogical support to university teachers.

Background to the Centres of Excellence in Teaching and Learning initiative

In 2015 the University Grants Commission (UGC) and the British Council in Bangladesh proposed a network of Centres of Excellence in Teaching and Learning (CETLs), to be based in six public universities—Dhaka, Rajshahi, Chittagong, Khulna, Jahangirnagar, and Bangladesh Agricultural University—and a seventh at the private BRAC University (British Council 2020). By establishing a center in each institution, the UGC and British Council hoped to establish a regular program of academic professional development, which would help to raise the standards of teaching in each university. The expectation was that these seven centers would become hubs of expertise, providing support to other universities in their respective regions. Three other private universities subsequently joined the initiative: American International University-Bangladesh, Green University, and the University of Liberal Arts Bangladesh.

Many lecturers are appointed after master's level study and move straight from student to teacher without any formal training (Raqib 2019). Before the CETL initiative, there was no systemwide approach for university teachers, except for a program offered since 2007 by the Graduate Training Institute of the Bangladesh

Agricultural University for public university staff, spanning a range of teaching and research skills. Since 2006, BRAC University had offered a Postgraduate Certificate in Higher Education program for its staff, and since 2013, Green University had developed its own in-house professional development program. Quality assurance systems at the national and institutional level were established as part of the HEQEP, but this did not directly cover teaching practice. As a result, university teaching was of varying quality. Typically, it focused heavily on content with little orientation to learners' needs and delivered primarily through presentation-based lectures to large classes—in some extreme cases of 200 or more students—and with little use of digital technology.

Part of the British Council's inspiration for the Bangladesh initiative was a leadership development program in Afghanistan. The Afghanistan project made use of remote mentoring to support a cohort of university leaders, evolving from an individual training initiative, to operate more strategically through the establishment of Centers of Excellence in Quality Assurance. The shift in emphasis recognized that a strategic change initiative with more tangible outcomes was likely to offer a stronger platform for management and leadership training (Parvin 2020). The British Council originally conceived the Bangladesh project was as a management and leadership program, however, early discussions identified the lack of a professional development program for university teachers to be a major problem, and it was decided to focus on teaching quality.

The British Council's project drew on the experience of similar centers in the UK, which have played various roles to support the teaching practice of university teaching staff, offering training and mentoring, support to make use of digital learning resources, and in some cases, running postgraduate certificates in higher education teaching. Advanced Higher Education (Advance HE) has developed a national training program for higher education staff, mapped to the Advance HE Development Pathway (Advance HE UK 2020), and operates a voluntary UK Professional Standards Framework for higher education teaching staff, which provides a "comprehensive set of professional standards and guidelines for everyone involved in teaching and supporting learning in [higher education] (HE)" (UKPSF 2011).

While the CETL project brought expertise from the UK, it drew on significant Bangladeshi expertise and experience. Notable is the work of BRAC, which had established its professional development center in 2006, and later the work of Green University. BRAC began with a series of short training sessions for staff and went on to develop a multiday residential course and later a 3-month certificate course for academic teachers (Box 3). The certificate course required academics to complete an intensive 4-day preparatory course before entering the classroom, and then spend 3 hours a week in further professional development sessions.

Box 3:   The Centres of Excellence in Teaching and Learning Project

What did the Centres of Excellence in Teaching and Learning project set out to do and how?
The Centres of Excellence in Teaching and Learning (CETL) project worked on two fronts in parallel. The first dimension was "structural," focusing on establishing the centers and incorporating them into the organogram of each institution. The second dimension was a curriculum and the skills to deliver it. The structural dimension was relatively easy to achieve. Each public university was able to cover the costs for a part time director and deputy director from the University Grants Commission's (UGC's) core grant to the institution, and these became established in the universities' formal structures. However, they had no further project funding to draw on. This was in contrast to the relatively well-funded Institutional Quality Assurance Cells (IQAC) which were being established under the auspices of the Higher Education Quality Enhancement Project (HEQEP).

Developing a curriculum for the CETLs

A six-module curriculum was designed to provide a broad orientation to academic practice, covering: (i) teaching pedagogy, (ii) modern approaches to teaching and learning, (iii) research methodology and ethics and optimizing the

continued on next page

Box 3   *continued*

use of e-resources, (iv) quality assurance processes and practice, (v) language and communication skills, and (vi) fundamentals of information technology (IT) and advanced IT skills.

Participants felt that there was also little to give new staff the sense of having joined the university so an induction module was developed, to introduce new staff to the structures and systems of the institution and developing a sense of accountability to the university and its students.

Delivering the Program

Each CETL took the core curriculum and adapted it to its own needs and institutional context. Progress has been mixed across the centers. Public universities have experienced significant operational challenges. Although there was funding to cover the director and deputy posts and staff, some struggled to secure proper offices and facilities and encountered bureaucratic obstacles in securing the budgets needed to run the center and regular training programs. In most cases, the directors and their deputies did not have significant time to support the work of the center, as these were additional roles on top of their existing academic and administrative roles. Some CETLs were able to run the full curriculum, while others struggled to do so and were limited to short occasional workshops as funding and the availability of facilitators allowed. CETLs in Dhaka, Jahangirnagar, and Khulna were the most active, conducting regular workshops and training sessions; Rajshahi started well, but struggled to deliver a regular program of training and support to faculty.

Developing the curriculum enabled the group to consider how it could be delivered and resourced. It became clear early on that there was a lack of resource people with the expertise and experience to do this within the country. A group of teaching staff from the six CETLs was trained at the Graduate Teaching Institute at the Bangladesh Agricultural University to create a pool of resource persons. However, the CETLs have found it difficult to identify appropriately skilled trainers with expertise in higher education pedagogy. They have also been impacted by changes in senior leadership, resulting in shifting levels of support for their work.

One of the most active centers was at Khulna University. It framed the center's work as a process of peer learning with and between teaching staff about different pedagogies, rather than prescribing an approach. It used the core curriculum to develop a three-module course that ran from January to December. Resource people were drawn from among senior faculty. While they were not all familiar with pedagogical theory, they were well-regarded teachers and popular with students. Each undertook an orientation session before the workshop, through which the CETL team communicated their desire to "sit and share experience" with lecturers, rather than to "teach and train" them. In this way, they encouraged junior lecturers to develop their philosophy and style of teaching.[a]

The first day of Khulna's course was significantly lecture-based, but subsequent sessions were run in more of a workshop mode, with group work and practical elements on preparing course outlines and delivering a model lecture, sharing of experiences in peer seminars, and group work. Courses were followed by a series of seminars covering assessment, dialogue with students, peer observation. A peer observation process was also introduced, with expectations that each member of staff would both observe a colleague and be observed once a year.[b]

Nurturing a network of CETLs

British Council consultants traveled to Bangladesh twice a year, to bring the CETLs together for a central workshop.[c] However, the project had no central leadership or mentoring team to support the CETLs in the intervening months. Workshops were co-facilitated by the consultants, who were involved with a Leicester CETL on genetics education. The intention was to model ways of facilitating learning through the sessions. The consultants delivered sessions on how teaching and learning and academic development were supported and managed at Leicester and took a facilitative approach to encourage participants to think about which elements of the Leicester approach might be relevant and feasible within the Bangladeshi context. Rather than importing solutions from the United Kingdom (UK), the aim was to use these examples to stimulate thinking about how the issues might be approached in Bangladesh, the barriers that participants would encounter, and how these could be overcome.

continued on next page

Box 3   *continued*

Through these visits, each of the core CETLs was connected to a UK university. The universities of Greenwich, Leicester, Liverpool John Moores, Loughborough, Southampton Solent, and University College London have all been involved, and several visits were arranged for Bangladesh CETL staff to the UK. Bangladeshi colleagues were also encouraged to explore the UK's professional accreditation framework, offered by Advance HE (formerly the Higher Education Academy), as a way to support their personal development and growth and to understand how a professional framework could be developed to underpin wider change in the Bangladeshi system.

[a] Parvin, Interview: Centre of Excellence in Teaching and Learning, Khulna University.
[b] Centre of Excellence in Teaching and Learning, "Guidelines for Peer Observation."
[c] Hank Williams, often with the late Mark Goodwin from Leicester University.

Source: Compiled by the authors.

Navigating the Politics of the Higher Education System

The project—as with other initiatives to strengthen the higher education system in Bangladesh—was inevitably affected by the politics of the system. Public universities tend to operate in a reactive mode, often responding to episodes of student unrest. Both the staff and student body tend to split along party lines and vice chancellors in all of Bangladesh's universities are appointed for a 4-year term by the president, who holds the position of chancellor. As a result, the role of the vice chancellor is significantly politicized. Alongside a funding model that does not create obvious pressures for change, this means that the focus of universities—and their senior leadership—is often dealing with short-term issues, rather than the longer-term strategic planning that the CETLs required.

Several CETLs have had to navigate this political space. While the CETL directors generally did not want to undertake the role on a fulltime basis—as this would have taken them away from other academic work—they also did not want the vice chancellors to make a fulltime appointment, fearing this would lead to its subsequent politicization as has happened to other leadership positions.

During the life of the project, the UGC also sought to become an independent organization. This was resisted by the Ministry of Education who wanted to retain direct control over the higher education system, but it created further tensions. The UGC's preference was for a national training college, while the project team advocated a model like the UK professional standards framework and fellowship. The latter was less attractive to the UGC since it did not create a clear institutional body, the responsibility for which would have strengthened its role.

Accountability and Recognition within Higher Education

Bangladesh has many excellent academics and the system produces many able graduates, but a lack of accountability mechanisms within public universities—or recognition for good teaching—means that good teaching is typically the result of personal motivation and effort by academic staff (Rahman et al. 2019). This has been a challenge for many of the CETLs within the public higher education system. The roles and responsibilities of teaching staff are not clearly defined, teaching is not monitored or evaluated, and there is no mechanism for student feedback, so there is little direct incentive for teachers to improve their practice (Parvin 2019). Lecturers do not expect to be challenged about their teaching practices and attempts to do so are seen as an infringement of academic freedom (Parvin 2020). Academic staff are promoted to higher grades based on years of service and publications: a promotion from assistant professor to associate professor requires 4 years' experience and four publications, but there is no measure of performance and publications may not be assessed, which means malpractice is not uncommon.

The IQACs—as part of the HEQEP—introduced new quality assurance mechanisms, such as departmental self-assessment reports. However, there was little scrutiny of these, and in some cases, they were simply produced to meet a milestone and to secure the funding attached to it. There was also some confusion between the roles of the CETLs and the IQACs. Some of the IQACs were uncomfortable with another unit developing a mandate for teaching quality within the institution. The greatest progress was made where the Institutional Quality Assurance Cell (IQAC) and CETLs were able to collaborate.

Outcomes of the CETL Initiative

A lack of systematic institutional evaluation means it is difficult to make firm statements about impact, but accounts from several CETLs, alongside a formal evaluation commission by the British Council, suggest some positive results. CETLs were reportedly well-regarded by established teachers, training participants, and administrators; raised awareness of the importance of teaching and learning throughout institutions; and some were credited with unifying more sporadic attempts to improve quality. The most significant impact of the project seems to be a heightened awareness of the importance of teaching quality and pedagogy, and the responsibilities of teachers to ensure that students are engaged and learning. However, not all training modeled active and learner-centered approaches. There was often limited follow-up support or mentoring, and tension emerged between the academic credibility of a lecture and the practical value of a skills development program. Commitment from vice chancellors and senior leaders has also been variable (Williams 2020).

Achievements of the Public Universities

At the University of Dhaka, all six core modules have been established, with 25 workshops run for around 1,500 academic teachers, as well as further workshops for other university staff (during the period covered by the evaluation). Positive outcomes are reported about awareness of teaching practices, IT skills, understanding of rules and regulations and ethical principles, and greater degrees of cultural and gender-related sensitivity. The evaluation notes that the university's Institute of Education and Research played an important role in providing pedagogical expertise, however, Institute staff also tended to prefer delivering lectures rather than running training, and feedback was mixed (Williams 2020). Having trained many academic staff, the Dhaka CETL now needs to develop more advanced, tailored programs, and evaluate its impact on student learning.

The CETL at Khulna University held 10 workshops, engaging 445 members of teaching staff from across the university's 28 disciplines (faculties) as well as a series of strategic and policy level discussions. While it was difficult to identify concrete outcomes, mindset shifts were observed; teachers participating in the programs felt better motivated, and there was evidence of more student-centered teaching emerging with new teaching and assessment methods being introduced (Parvin 2020). The CETL initiative has helped to raise awareness of pedagogical theories, improve the processes of course design and planning, strengthened assessment practices, and encouraged more effective engagement between students and teachers. Khulna also involved three other regional universities in its training program. However, changes in leadership and the lack of sufficient skilled trainers and facilitators have limited its ability to sustain and deepen support since 2018.

The CETL at Jahangirnagar University reports similar successes to those of Dhaka and Khulna—increased awareness, better course design and planning, improvements in assessment and engagement between staff and students—and has also benefited from strong leadership and its training expertise. Rajshahi University's CETL started well, with an induction program held twice, receiving excellent feedback both times. It also started to play the role of a regional hub by welcoming newly recruited faculty from universities of the North Bengal region. However, administrative challenges mean it has struggled to remain active.

The CETL at Bangladesh Agricultural University was slower to be established due to confusion about how it would be integrated into existing university structures (alongside the existing Graduate Training Institute). The center at the University of Chittagong is noted to be less active—due to resource constraints—having run a limited number of workshops. The Shahjalal University of Science and Technology was not one of the original centers, but has been encouraged by the project to establish its CETL and was to be invited to join the program in 2020.

Achievements of the Private Universities

The private universities have developed more active CETLs. Their contexts are, however, significantly different. Funding structures have allowed them to respond differently, and smaller class sizes mean they can offer more interactive teaching.

BRAC University had a Professional Development Centre—established several years before the CETL initiative—and was able to draw on its funds and facilities during the project. The center runs between seven and 13 sessions each semester and has made participation in training provided by the center mandatory for all teaching staff as part of its Certificate in Teaching Strategies for Higher Education. In return, staff are relieved from teaching one course during the semester in which they undertake the program. Career progression for academic staff has thus become linked to participation in the program. Supported by its Technology Enhanced Education Unit, BRAC has been able to introduce lecturers to more advanced techniques and methods, such as gamification to engage students, and assessment skills and tools. It has also built a pool of trainers.

Green University has invested significantly in its teaching and learning since 2013; its Vice Chancellor was previously Pro Vice Chancellor at BRAC and had been instrumental in establishing its Center. Green has made the completion of an initial training program mandatory and successful participation (following an examination) is a prerequisite to be confirmed as a full-time member of staff. Staff going through the program follow classes and submit a syllabus and lesson plans and micro-teaching exercises (teaching a topic in the presence of peers). They are expected to develop a personal teaching philosophy, prepare a teaching portfolio, and produce a series of reflective pieces following their teaching. By spreading learning sessions over a longer period, the Green model has also enabled staff to practice what they have learned. Green also organized an open training course, which proved popular.

The University of Liberal Arts has established a CETL and has used this as a basis to assess needs and provide training, both the general modules developed by the project and its own more specialized sessions. It runs at least one session a month and hosted a conference in 2019 on quality in higher education, indicating the importance it has accorded to addressing these issues. It plans to develop a postgraduate certification program in teaching and leadership. The director of its center was a pedagogy expert and running the center has been made a core rather than additional responsibility.

Establishment of a Federation of Private Universities

Following the success of Green's open training program, the vice chancellors of Green, University of the Liberal Arts, North South University, Independent University, and Asia Pacific University came together to discuss a collaborative approach to academic development. It decided to offer a shared certificate course—which was launched in 2017—by a federation of 11 private universities, offering courses each semester open to both private and public university staff. The group also organizes an annual conference on teaching and learning, to bring experts from outside Bangladesh into conversations with its faculty and leadership.

Outcomes for Teachers

Lecturers interviewed by the evaluators were generally positive about the relevance and value of the modules. There is no quantitative data, and feedback is aggregated, so it is not possible to determine differences across institutions.

The induction was felt to be valuable to help them to understand the regulations and operating norms of their institutions and their responsibilities as teachers.

The module on modern pedagogical approaches helped to orient new teachers to foundational theories and concepts, lesson planning, dealing with students in a classroom situation, and assessment strategies.

The module on modern teaching and learning was valued for introducing concepts of student-centered learning, and for introducing lecturers to new digital tools, though the limits of university ICT infrastructure and facilities were constraining factors in making use of these.

The most positive feedback seems to be for a module focusing on research methods. This contributed directly to academics' professional progression by helping them to understand research and analytical methods and approaches to academic writing and publishing.

A module on quality assurance helped academics become more conscious of their accountability as teachers and the need to develop their teaching skills.

A module on IT skills was reportedly valued by most of those trained; the least valued module was one on language and communication skills.

Impact on university teachers and their relationships with the university

The evaluation report identifies impact in nine areas, though the evidence is slim in some of these, and many are focused on greater awareness of approaches rather than improvements in teaching practice:

(i)   The development of a "teacher identity," helping lecturers to understand their roles and responsibilities, and to develop their own style of teaching.
(ii)   Becoming part of the university and its culture and understanding its rules and processes.
(iii)   Awareness of the value of more engaged teaching methods, including group work and role play.
(iv)   Familiarity with concepts such as outcome-based teaching and competency-based learning, and some of the theories underpinning these.
(v)   Support teachers to develop their skills without fees or other barriers.
(vi)   Developing additional technical skills, including IT, research and writing skills, information literacy, and knowledge of publishing practices.
(vii)   A perception by teachers that they will be more highly regarded internationally and will open further opportunities.
(viii) Ethical consciousness, including an awareness of conflicts of interests, approaches to assessment, bias and subjectivity, and how to navigate sensitive topics.
(ix)   Individuals feeling more accountable in their roles as teachers.

Lessons
University Level

A need to extend and deepen the support offered. Initial training has shown signs of success, but as lecturers complete the introductory modules, they will require more tailored or advanced support.

Lecturers need support to move from theory to practice. Lecturers need more time to internalize what they learn, and more structured support and mentoring between workshops to put it into practice.

The assessment was missing in the initial approach to pedagogy: The project did not focus significantly on assessment processes, with implications for how teachers and students responded.

Connecting teaching and research reflected professional concerns. Research practices were incorporated into the core curriculum. This gave lecturers something which was immediately valuable to their academic careers and progression.

Senior academic champions can play important roles. Senior professors who championed CETLs and encouraged junior academics to participate played a powerful mobilizing function. In contrast, a lack of senior support, or leadership changes has affected the fortunes and ongoing success of the CETLs.

Training lecturers at cost and scale requires a pool of local, expert facilitators. Many centers were limited in their ability to mount training programs by a lack of local pedagogy experts, and the inability to afford the costs of bringing resource people and trainers from abroad. Academic hierarchies meant that only professors could be recruited as resource people, creating a lag in the ability to recruit new facilitators from CETL participants.

Improving quality is a matter of culture as much as management. While quality is often approached through regulatory or management processes, it depends significantly on shifting cultures and norms within institutions, and the attitudes of teachers, students, and administrators.

Network Level

Face-to-face training was preferred over "professional dialogue." A preference was observed for a more intensive face to face workshop mode of support, that offered practical training and learning to CETL teams, instead of a "dialogue mode" of support through peer exchanges with UK universities.

A central leadership function is needed to drive the initiative. The higher education system is relatively fragmented. There is little to keep the CETL network together, and some form of central leadership is likely to be needed, to coordinate learning and the maintenance of standards across the centers.

National Policy

Projects with modest budgets may struggle to gain traction alongside major donor investments. The initiative was designed to be a low-cost intervention to improve teaching quality. The CETLs' ability to sustain their core programs was constrained by a lack of resources and budget. In an environment with large scale donor-funded interventions like the HEQEP initiative, it can become difficult for financially modest initiatives to gain traction.

Support is needed over a longer duration. While absolute cost may not be a criterion for success, a longer period of support is likely to be needed to support a process of change which, in a complex and politicized higher education system, frequently impacted by changes in policy and leadership, will take time.

CETLs encouraged attitudinal and cultural change, but without links to promotion and reward systems progress was limited. The lack of mechanisms to reward and incentivize good teaching is noted in the CETLs in public universities and is a notable feature in private institutions where teacher accreditation was often dependent on participation in a professional development program. It is likely to be difficult to encourage wider institutional change if staff continue to be able to progress to higher academic ranks, regardless of the quality of teaching.

Capacity and resources are needed at multiple levels and it can be difficult to determine the most suitable sequencing of these. Many of the longer-term investments made in the country's higher education system have focused on infrastructure and facilities, which are necessary, but insufficient to improve quality. At the same time, efforts to improve teaching and learning quality, in environments where infrastructure is limited can also struggle. Smaller scale changes and improvements may need to be piloted, to move the system in the direction of better quality, but before more ambitious programs of change, with more significant investment, can be successfully implemented, at scale.

Hong Kong, China—Supporting Professional Learning of Blended and Online Learning to Enhance University Teaching and Learning

Authors: Danlin Yang, Yuen Man Tang, and Cher Ping Lim,* The Education University of Hong Kong

*Corresponding author

Introduction
Issues and Challenges of Professional Learning for Blended and Online Learning in Universities

Professional learning of blended and online learning for teachers in many universities focuses on the features and functions of the online learning tools without explaining how these tools could be used within their courses to enhance teaching and learning (Porter and Graham 2016). This focus on the online learning tools may not prepare university teachers adequately to use these tools in their courses and transform their practices (Meyer 2014). These professional learning sessions may be conducted as one-off workshops that may not meet the ongoing professional learning needs of university teachers as they need to be supported when using such online learning tools in their courses (van As 2018). The lack of ongoing professional support for university teachers as they attempt to implement blended and online learning may discourage university teachers to engage in such practices (Vaughan 2010; Kennedy et al. 2011; Herman 2012). At the same time, many of these professional learning sessions adopt the one-size-fits-all approach that may not meet the diverse professional learning needs of university teachers.

Given these challenges, it is crucial to engage university teachers in ongoing professional learning to harness online technologies for blended and online learning in their courses. Based on a grassroots approach toward professional learning in a faculty at a university in Hong Kong, China, this chapter discusses how university teachers could be supported in their professional learning of blended and online learning to enhance the quality of teaching and learning.

Practical Implications

The grassroots approach toward professional learning offers ongoing professional learning opportunities for university teachers to build their capacity for blended and online learning in their courses. The ongoing professional support from peers and specialists provides university teachers with a conducive environment to explore and experiment with blended and online learning in their courses. With an emphasis on the pedagogical use of the online tools, the grassroots approach scaffolds university teachers to reflect on their existing practices and examine how the online tools could be used in their courses to enhance the quality of teaching and learning.

Grassroots Approach Toward Professional Learning

The Education University of Hong Kong strives for quality teaching and learning, and impactful research locally and internationally. The Faculty of Education and Human Development (FEHD) is one of the three faculties in the Education University of Hong Kong and consists of six departments. It is committed to drive and support quality teaching and learning, and to enable staff and students to realize their full potential. Blended and online learning is recognized as one of the key drivers for teaching and learning quality enhancement in FEHD. The faculty leaders, including the dean, associate deans, heads of department, and the departmental chairs of the teaching and learning committee, are committed to drive and support blended and online learning in FEHD (Laurillard 2005; Porter and Graham 2016; Moskal et al. 2013). When leaders demonstrate such commitment, university teachers are more likely to engage in blended and online learning practices (Graham et al. 2013). The grassroots approach toward professional learning and support is well-aligned with this leadership commitment to enhancing quality teaching and learning.

With the support of the faculty leadership, the Technology-Enhanced Learning Hub (TEL-Hub) was established in 2015 to build the capacity of the teachers in FEHD for blended and online learning, develop online teaching and learning resources, and explore emerging technologies. To achieve these aims, TEL-Hub adopted the grassroots approach by:

  (i)   providing just-in-time professional learning and support;
  (ii) offering customized professional learning sessions;
  (iii) harnessing the experiences and expertise of blended and online learning ambassadors who are the leading blended and online learning practitioners in each department in FEHD;
  (iv) developing and providing access to online professional learning and support resources; and
  (v)   providing teaching team-based professional learning and support.

Just-In-Time Professional Learning and Support

University teachers need just-in-time professional learning and support as they explore how blended and online learning could be an integral part of their courses (Herman 2012). TEL-Hub offers individualized consultation sessions for the teachers to adopt blended and online learning in their courses. The initial session might involve the teachers discussing their initial ideas of the blended and online learning activities with the TEL-Hub staff who are blended and online learning specialists. The ongoing consultation sessions allow the TEL-Hub staff to engage the teachers as part of a professional learning community (MacDonald and Campbell 2012). The TEL-Hub staff usually discuss the feasibility of the idea with the teachers, collaborate with them to realize the ideas, and introduce the teachers to online learning tools to facilitate the blended and online learning activities. The teachers then design and implement blended and online learning into their courses. Just-in-time support is provided for the teachers by the TEL-Hub staff during design and implementation. Just-in-time professional learning coupled with support from design to implementation are critical to engaging university teachers in adopting blended and online learning in their courses (Moskal et al. 2013).

Customized Professional Learning Sessions

As part of the grassroots approach, professional learning sessions were customized to accommodate the diverse learning needs of the teachers in FEHD (Buchanan et al. 2013). Professional learning sessions must build the capacity of teachers to adopt the online tools in their courses instead of focusing on the features of online learning tools (Gregory and Salmon 2013). Therefore, unlike the one-off workshops focusing on the online tools, TEL-Hub runs 30-minute hands-on workshops regularly (three times a week) that explore the design and development of blended and online learning activities enabled by online learning tools. The workshops aim to build teacher confidence to adopt online tools in their courses and develop their capacities to design and implement blended and online learning activities with a pedagogical focus.

The hands-on workshops consist of two integral parts: the hands-on practice of online tools, and discussion of how the online tools could be used within the course to enhance student learning engagement. During the workshop, the teachers learn how to use the tools as a student, and how to design meaningful online activities with the tools as a teacher. As a student, for example, they might engage in online small group discussions on Padlet, an online collaboration platform. As a teacher, they might explore how to design online activities on Padlet to provide students with meaningful learning experiences. These hands-on workshops provide the university teachers with both the student and teacher perspectives; the university teachers then are more likely to be aware of the importance of pedagogy with the technology, and the potential of technology to enhance student engagement. Therefore, they may be less reluctant to use online tools for blended and online learning in their courses (Gregory and Salmon 2013).

Blended and Online Learning Ambassadors

To support and sustain professional learning in FEHD, the blended and online learning ambassadors' scheme was initiated in 2015. The ambassadors were teachers who were front-runners of blended and online learning practices from the six departments in FEHD. These ambassadors were offered one-course relief from their teaching workload to allow them to spend more time supporting the professional learning of their colleagues in the department and faculty. They were designated to share their practices in and across departments and provide peer support for colleagues within their department (Porter and Graham 2016; Vaughan and Garrison 2006). The ambassadors shared their blended and online learning practices, and how they addressed the challenges encountered when designing and implementing the activities.

The sharing sessions provided vivid examples of how blended and online learning activities could be adopted. Moreover, they provided evidence on how their students benefited from such learning experiences in the courses. At the departmental level—in collaboration with TEL-Hub—the ambassadors organized sharing sessions with follow-up hands-on workshops to discuss blended and online learning practices relevant to the courses in the department with their colleagues. The sharing sessions usually consisted of four parts. First, the ambassadors introduced the courses and their previous teaching experience with online technologies. Second, they shared the online learning tools they adopted in the courses, why the tools were selected for the courses, and how they integrated these tools into the courses. Third, they showed the impacts on student learning engagement and outcomes. Finally, they reflected on the challenges and impact of their blended and online learning practices.

Such sharing sessions within the same department enabled the teachers to relate to their teaching practices as they were more likely to teach similar courses as the ambassadors. They were also more likely to be convinced by the evidence shared by colleagues (ambassadors) from their department regarding the feasibility of online tools in the courses, and the positive impact of blended and online learning on student engagement. With the support from the ambassadors and the TEL-Hub staff, the teachers learned how the online tools shared in the sessions could be adopted in their courses. More importantly, they are more likely to perceive the potential of blended and online learning and take up this potential to enhance the quality of teaching and learning in their universities.

Apart from the sharing sessions and workshops in FEHD, the blended and online learning ambassadors were committed to cultivating a blended and online learning culture across the faculties in the university. To expand the influence and engage more university teachers, videos of the ambassadors' blended learning practices were recorded, and their experiences were shared in different university teaching and learning events. The types of sharing can provide ongoing opportunities for university teachers to exchange their ideas and experiences as a professional learning community that will support and sustain professional learning for blended and online learning beyond faculty and cultivate a blended and online learning culture (Boelens et al. 2018; Napier et al. 2011). Such a professional learning community allows the teachers in the faculty to continuously learn, reflect and contribute to their teaching practices.

Professional Learning and Support Online Resources

Another crucial component is the online resources to support professional learning for the teachers. The online resources are accessible anytime and anywhere so that the teachers can learn at their own pace (Torrisi-Steele and Drew 2013; Moskal et al. 2013). There were three sets of blended and online learning resources to meet the diverse needs of university teachers. First, the Blended Learning Professional Learning Resources focused on Moodle, the main learning management system at the university. Compared with the existing Moodle technical resources, this set of professional learning resources specifies how each Moodle feature could be adopted for blended and online learning activities. It consisted of the features of Moodle activities and resources, short step-by-step video guides, and good practices for adopting the features to facilitate blended and online learning. This set of professional learning resources has been regularly updated to keep pace with Moodle upgrades and to address the suggestions of the teachers.

Second, an online collection of selected emerging online technologies was created to keep the teachers updated with the emerging technologies. This collection serves as a platform to inform teachers about the potential of free online tools and how these could be adopted in their courses. There is also a need to provide concrete evidence of the benefits of blended and online learning for the quality enhancement of learning and teaching. The third set of professional learning resources is the sharing of promising blended and online learning practices by university teachers. These promising practices illustrate the pedagogical opportunities provided by online technologies for quality enhancement.

These three sets of professional learning resources were a collaborative effort of the TEL-Hub staff and the teachers in FEHD as a professional learning community for blended and online learning. The university teachers would learn from the resources to explore the pedagogical opportunities provided by the online technologies. At the same time, they could share their experiences as peer support and resources. The ongoing professional learning meets the diverse professional learning needs of the teachers and supports the sustainability of the quality of the accessible professional learning resources on blended and online learning.

Teaching Team-Based Professional Learning and Support

The customized professional learning and support for blended and online learning contributed to the capacity building of university teachers in adopting online technologies, and the development of the professional learning community for blended and online learning in FEHD. The TEL-Hub staff started collaborating with the faculty e-learning innovation team in 2018 to take a step forward for the grassroots approach. Online learning packages were developed for courses that were taught by many teachers to provide more blended and online learning opportunities for students and support them to have a more meaningful learning experience (Vaughan 2010). TEL-Hub staff worked together with the faculty e-learning innovation team, and the course teaching team to redesign blended and online learning activities. With the professional learning and support offered by TEL-Hub staff, the whole course teaching teams were presented with more opportunities to redesign the blended and online learning activities with the newly developed online learning packages (Boelens et al. 2018).

Implications for Practice

How could the grassroots approach be applied to developing countries?

The support of the leadership is crucial in the adoption of the grassroots approach toward professional learning.

Given the complexity of blended and online learning with ever-changing technologies, professional learning and support need to be ongoing so that university teachers have sufficient support when encountering challenges.

Professional learning and support need to focus on the pedagogical opportunities of online technologies, rather than on the features of the online tools.

It is necessary to provide cost-effective online tools that enable more university teachers to adopt and adapt to the blended and online learning approach.

Republic of Korea—Teacher Professional Development in the University

Author: Meekyung Shin, education specialist, ADB

Background

Unlike the emphasis on the importance of professional development of teachers in K–12 education, the discussion on improving teachers' educational capacity in universities began relatively late. In the case of the higher education of the Republic of Korea (ROK), the teaching capacity of teachers depended on the efforts of individual universities and professors, without government intervention until 2000. Whether universities teach well had not been an important agenda in the Korean higher education policies. The reputation of universities was mainly determined by the number of excellent high school students and the number of professors who published high-quality research papers. Discussions on the quality of university education programs were lacking, and there was little policy intervention in the teaching quality of professors.

Since 2000, enrollment for higher education has expanded. However, there is a mismatch between college education and the country's industrial needs, resulting in a high unemployment rate for college graduates. It has thus become important for universities to provide education to meet the needs of industry. Furthermore, the Fourth Industrial Revolution has necessitated the creation of human resources that lead to innovation.[7] Discussion, team projects, communication with students among the classes, how quality technology is used in teaching and educating, and industrial cooperation have become important.

In response, universities in ROK have begun to establish an independent organization to support instructors' teaching capacities. In 1997, the first Center for Teaching and Learning (CTL) was established in Inha University. In 2001, six universities—including Seoul National University, Sungkyunkwan University, and Yeonsei University—established the Korean Association of Centers for Teaching and Learning with six members. The association has enhanced the activities of CTLs through cooperation and sharing of information, and it has grown into a consultative body with 156 member schools as of 2012. Since the establishment of the association, enthusiastic professors continuously highlight the importance of teaching competency of university instructors and have asked the government to provide administrative and financial support to universities to establish CTLs to improve the quality of university education.

---

[7]   "The Fourth Industrial Revolution can be described as the advent of "cyber-physical systems" involving entirely new capabilities for people and machines" (Nicholas Davis, World Economic Forum Global Agenda, 19 January 2006, accessed 8 April 2021).

The Government of the Republic of Korea has begun to pay attention not only to research capacity, but also to the quality of education. The government included university efforts to improve the quality of education in the accreditation criteria for the second university accreditation (2001–2006) and launched a series of financial support projects that focus on improving the quality of university education.

These efforts were recognized by the government in 2008 when it launched a national financial support project for university education innovation. It led to fostering CTLs at many universities. CTLs organize various programs such as teaching methodology support, learning support, e-learning and educational media support, and education policy research.

Another critical government policy for fostering an education-oriented university was to initiate cooperation between industry and academe. The government has promoted many projects to strengthen university-industry cooperation, adapt university education to industrial demand, and has appointed industry field experts as faculty members. The introduction of professors who are evaluated by their performance in the industry rather than research has played a decisive role in addressing the mismatch between industry and academe.

Activities of Centers for Teaching and Learning

CTLs became centers for teaching improvement and learning and organized various types of training that included special lectures, workshops, professors' study groups, class consulting, teaching portfolios, and developing e-learning programs.

Teaching experts were invited to improve the professor-experts' teaching skills and knowledge in teaching methods. The teacher experts lectured on topics that included general teaching methods, English, discussion classes, problem-based learning presentations, microteaching, eLearning, and smart media usage.

Workshops were organized on teaching methods for new professors, multimedia utilization, English workshops, as well as customized workshops by major and subject. Professor study groups and teaching clubs support the professors' community in teaching methods. These study groups provide research funds so that professors can conduct research activities to improve the quality of lectures through small education research groups.

Class recording analysis and consulting services consist of lecture recording and analysis, and analysis of teaching methods. The aim is to self-diagnose lectures and provide the feedback necessary for improvement.

Teaching portfolio development supports teaching capacity by providing professors themselves with opportunities for systematic and comprehensive management and reflection on the teaching process and results. Schools that implement teaching portfolios select and award excellent teaching portfolios, publish them as best practice books, and share them. Other programs include mentoring groups between new and incoming professors to observe each other's classes and share feedback; or running various programs tailored to the characteristics of particular universities, such as holding professor-learning method research contests (Box 4).

Intervention

Beginning in 2000, the government used teaching and learning infrastructure as an assessment criterion in university accreditation and launched financial support projects for universities. The government started the Advancement of College Education (ACE) project, which invested up to $2.5 million for 3 years to selected universities. To be chosen as an ACE University, universities had to create programs for better education.

Box 4:   Case Example–Pusan National University

The Teaching and Learning Faculty Academy of Pusan National University* supports all the professors in teaching methods and strategic competencies for student participation-oriented classes through online and offline lectures, workshops, and consulting programs and expands opportunities for participation.

1. Activities
    1.1.   Lectures on various teaching methods and teaching strategies
    1.2.   Course Topics: Teaching Methods and Applications, Educational Philosophy and Teaching Strategies, Student Communication Skills, Teaching English Teaching (168 lecture programs about teaching methods in 2016–2018)
    1.3.   Consulting through class diagnosis and improvement feedback
        1.3.1.   consulting process: class video recording, self-diagnosis writing, interviewing, interview consulting, and curriculum development consulting (22 consulting services for consultants in 2017–2018)
    1.4.   Faculty research group activities
    1.5.   Research Topic: Development and Application of Teaching Method by Department (Flip Learning, PBL, Convergence Class), Development of Online Teaching Tips (21 teams and 48 participants in 2016–2018)

2. Administrative and institutional support for improving teaching capacity
    2.1.   Linked teaching education capacity and personnel evaluation: to reflect the efforts to enhance teaching capacity in the performance-based salary system
    2.2.   Set guidelines of self-operation standards for capacity improvement
    2.3.   Development of information system to support faculty professionalism
    2.4.   Inclusion of training participation information to faculty achievement management system and online program for the academic management system (62 classes in 2016–2018)

3. Effects
    3.1.   Participant professors' average grades of student lecture evaluation are higher than nonparticipant professors
    3.2.   Academic self-efficacy, class commitment, class participation, and learning satisfaction of students improved in the results of the pre- and post-survey
    3.3.   Observational findings show that learners have developed self-directed learning functions and are involved in more discussion instead of listening

Source: 2018 Annual Report Pusan National University Centre for Teaching and Learning.

University Accreditation

The second university accreditation was conducted in 2000. As opposed to the first university accreditation (1994–2000)—which emphasized the improvement of social accountability of universities—the second university accreditation focused on teaching and learning conditions and included the development of teaching methodology and evaluation criteria. The government used evaluation indexes based on whether the university was classified as education-oriented, or research-oriented. Education-oriented universities could get accredited regardless of a professor's research performance, if the teaching and learning support system was well organized and operated effectively. The move made many universities establish CTLs and strengthen their functions.

The basis of the evaluation is to determine whether universities have dedicated organizations to improve classes and provide programs to improve the quality of classes. The results will clarify whether to secure dedicated organizations, the status of budget compilation and execution, the status of self-development of teaching and learning programs and data, and the performance of efforts to evaluate and improve programs. Owing to the accreditation, the number of CTLs in universities rapidly increased from 6 in 2001 to 156 in 2012.

Government Financial Support

By 2018, Korean universities were experiencing a sharp decline in the school-age population. In response to this, the government supported universities and implemented restructuring procedures for more autonomous reforms. Among them, the ACE project played a role in encouraging universities to strive to strengthen their educational capabilities by supporting them to develop tailor-made programs suited to their requirements. As universities became interested in developing education programs and improving educational conditions, the number of CTLs increased, which expanded activities for improving teaching quality. At the same time, the government encouraged a culture in which universities could assess their educational capabilities. Lower-rung universities were excluded from financial support funds and state scholarships. Because of comprehensive government efforts, universities strengthened their programs and the CTLs led the implementation of these policies.

The University Education Competency Enhancement Support Project was implemented in 2009 to support the strengthening of the overall educational capacity of ROK universities. In 2010, ACE was launched to support the development of models for undergraduate education, and in 2012, the Leaders in Industry-College Cooperation (LINC) project was launched to support the development of industrial-academic cooperation among universities. In 2016, the Program for Industrial Needs-Matched Education project was launched to reorganize the university curriculum and promote convergence, reflecting industrial demand in the era of the Fourth Industrial Revolution. Although each of these projects had a specific purpose, common areas they supported included the development of university education courses and innovation of teaching methods and various activities to strengthen teaching capabilities. Most of the programs were operated by centers for teaching in universities.

Industry-Academic Cooperation

To promote industry-academic cooperation sustainably, the government introduced industry expert practitioners as professors. The government prepared a plan to improve the system of university professors for promoting industry-academic cooperation in 2011 and revised the Higher Education Act to enable universities to hire industry practitioners as professors in the same year, which increased the number of professors to 5,726 by 2014.

Beginning in 2012, the number of industry practitioner professors increased sharply with the launching of the LINC project. LINC supported the university program of nurturing outstanding human resources and technological innovation that met the needs of industries. One of the criteria for selection into LINC was a university's number of industry-practitioner professors. Fifty universities were selected as participating schools in the LINC initiative. The goal was to reform college education systems, increase the employment rate, and promote the growth of local industries through industry-academic collaboration. The LINC project provided the budget to run key education programs such as hands-on experiments, on-site training, internships, and industry-academic contract majors.

The government also considered using retired employees—including chief executive officers of companies—as professors so that university education could reflect corporate needs and provide employment standards. These professors focused on (i) training human resources to meet the needs of industries and future industrial development, (ii) education for the creation and spread of new knowledge and technology, (iii) research and development, (iv) support for start-ups and employment, (v) transfer of technology to industries, and (vi) industry advice. These professors are evaluated on their industry performance and not just research alone. The introduction of this system served as an important opportunity to emphasize the education function as well as research.

Implications

Since 2000, the government and universities have been aware of the importance of universities that teach well and have implemented various policies that include the operation of CTLs and industry practitioner-professor system in personnel management. The government's interest in the education capacity of universities—which began relatively late compared with other advanced countries—and the spread of the establishment of CTLs in universities played an essential role in making universities think about educational activities as well as research activities.

Unlike the UK's setting of national standards for university education instructors and its systematic evaluation and education programs, and the United States' strengthening of teaching capacity through its efforts, ROK has undertaken indirect support measures such as including evaluation indicators in university certification evaluations and financial support projects.

The government supported the budget for education programs through the introduction of financial support projects and encouraged university efforts by including teaching and learning support conditions as the evaluation index of accreditation. With indirect support and the state's encouragement, university professors also established and operated the association of CTLs where they cooperate to develop its functions.

The government also created a system to hire teachers with experience in various industries. These professors played a major role in transforming university education into one that meets the demand of the workforce by guiding various educational activities that are not wholly based on research. The government promoted financial support projects to promote industry-academic cooperation and played a role in the selection of teachers focusing on industry-academic cooperation.

In the COVID-19 crisis, CTL has played a significant role in providing training and support for professors to record and upload online courses. Post-COVID-19, universities and the government are preparing the next steps to enable university CTLs to adapt to a new educational environment.

United Kingdom—The Teaching Excellence and Student Outcomes Framework

Author: Jonathan Harle, director of programs (International Network for Advancing Science and Policy [INASP], the United Kingdom).

Introduction

The Teaching Excellence and Student Outcomes Framework (TEF)—originally the Teaching Excellence Framework—was introduced by the Government of the United Kingdom (UK) in response to a concern that research was being privileged over teaching, and that measures were needed to push universities to improve the quality of teaching, alongside existing measures to incentivize and reward performance in research.[8]

The TEF was introduced into a sector that had established well-regarded mechanisms for ensuring the quality of the provision of higher education, and a history of support to higher education teachers to improve their professional practice. It was framed as a quality enhancement tool when first introduced, rather than as an addition to the quality assurance process. Since its introduction, the TEF has been the focus of significant debate within the education sector. An independent review was commissioned by the government in 2019 (Universities UK 2019). The report has yet to be released and its recommendations are not yet known, however, comments from the chair of the review indicate significant tensions within the sector (Dickinson 2019; Ashwin 2020).

Supporting Teaching and Learning in UK Higher Education Before the TEF

Before the introduction of the TEF, there were no formal measures for assessing and reporting on the quality of teaching at a national level. However, there were mechanisms to ensure that quality standards were maintained, and some support was available to higher education lecturers to strengthen their teaching practice.[9]

(i) The **Quality Assurance Agency** (QAA) was established in 1997 as an independent agency to ensure that academic standards are maintained. It does so through external peer review of the programs that universities offer against a quality code (UK Standing Committee for Quality Assessment and Quality Assurance Agency 2018), which sets common standards for UK higher education practice and includes an expectation that universities provide high quality teaching and learning support.

(ii) The **Institute for Learning and Teaching in Higher Education** was established in 2000, to accredit degree programs, commission research into teaching practices, and encourage innovation in teaching and learning practices. In parallel, the Learning and Teaching Support Network was established, a series of 24 subject centers to support the development of good practice and networks of practitioners. The institute and Learning and Teaching Support Network were merged to become the Higher Education Academy (HEA) in 2003, subsequently becoming Advance Higher Education (Advance HE) in 2018.

(iii) Advance HE (as the HEA) established a voluntary UK Professional Standards Framework for higher education teaching staff (Advance HE 2011), which provides a "comprehensive set of professional standards and guidelines for everyone involved in teaching and supporting learning in HE (higher education)," expressed as "Dimensions of Professional Practice." It offers a training program for HE staff, mapped to the Advance HE Development Pathway (Advance HE Development Pathway 2018) and teaching staff can become fellows, either through completion of a postgraduate certificate in higher education or academic practice or through an assessed portfolio (HEA 2020).

From 2000 to 2012 there were a series of well-regarded "subject centers" established under the HEA—based in university faculties—which offered discipline-focused support to academics across the UK. Advance higher education now organizes its work around four discipline clusters: arts and humanities, health and social care, social sciences, and science, technology, engineering, and mathematics (STEM).

---

[8]   Since 1992, there have been measures to assess research performance, initially through the Research Assessment Exercise, which subsequently became the Research Excellence Framework.

[9]   Higher education funding and associated policy and regulation in the UK are devolved to the administrations in Wales, Scotland, and Northern Ireland, and thus some of the measures introduced by the UK government in London apply only to English higher education institutions.

Introduction of the Teaching Excellence and Student Outcomes Framework

The TEF was formally introduced into the UK higher education system via the 2016 Higher Education and Research Bill (Department for Business, Innovation and Skills 2016a) and an Act of Parliament in 2017—following Green and White papers (Department for Business, Innovation and Skills 2016b)—and was noted to represent the most significant reform to higher education regulation in the UK in the preceding 25 years (Department for Business, Innovation and Skills 2016a). TEF was thus part of a wider phase of regulatory reform, which included the regulation and funding of research.

The TEF intended to "put in place reputational and financial incentives that will drive up the standard of teaching in all universities" and to put "clear, understandable information about outcomes in the hands of students" to enable them to make better decisions on where to study (Department for Business, Innovation and Skills 2016a). It specifically covers undergraduate teaching and has not yet been extended to include taught postgraduate degrees. The existing QAA quality standards set minimum thresholds for university provision in the UK; the TEF would, therefore, reward performance above the QAA baseline. While research had been funded on a quality basis for several decades, teaching had continued to be funded based on student numbers, so the TEF was also expected to introduce a quality-linked funding mechanism (Gunn 2018b). The TEF is administered by the Office for Students. It only applies to English higher education institutions, since those in Wales, Scotland, and Northern Ireland are regulated by their funding councils. However, institutions in the rest of the UK could participate voluntarily, and many chose to do so.

While there is no direct link between the results of the TEF and the funding that an institution receives from the government, the TEF is linked to the financing of higher education through the powers granted to universities to increase student fees. From 2012, universities were granted the freedom to charge variable fees of up to £9,000 per year; most opted to charge the full fee.[10] Policy makers reportedly felt that, while there was a variation in the quality of teaching being provided by universities, all had chosen to charge the maximum—many relying on established reputations and rankings—and variable fees had failed to differentiate the sector as the government had expected.

What did the TEF set out to do and how?

Aims of the Teaching Excellence and Student Outcomes Framework

In its specification for the TEF, the UK government outlined four aims (Department of Education, UK 2017):

   (i)   to ensure students were better informed about what and where they studied;
   (ii) to raise esteem for teaching within universities;
   (iii) to recognize and reward excellent teaching; and
   (iv) to ensure that HE better met the needs of business, industry, and the professions.

The government intended that a national ranking for teaching would help to reorient universities' investments toward teaching (rather than only toward research) and that the public branding of an institution as "gold," "silver," or "bronze" would create a pressure to adjust fees. It was reasoned that students—who had little information with which to make informed judgments—would be able to make better decisions in the "marketplace" about where to spend their money, and universities would be able to respond more appropriately to these decisions (National Audit Office, UK 2017). It would also enable the government to open up the HE market to new providers since it would displace the existing hierarchy of institutions and allow new providers to recruit students based on an objective measure of quality (Gunn 2018a).

---

[10] Fees of £1,000 per student per year were introduced in 1998 to 1999 and raised to £3,000 in 2004.

Table 3:   Teaching Excellence and Student Outcomes Framework Assessment

TEF Categories of Assessment	Metrics	Data
Teaching quality	Student satisfaction with teaching	National Student Survey
	Student satisfaction with assessment and feedback	National Student Survey
Learning environment	Student satisfaction with academic support	National Student Survey
	Student retention on courses	Higher Education Statistics Agency
Student outcomes and learning gain	Employment or further study (6 months after graduation)	Graduate Outcomes
	Highly skilled employment or further study (6 months after graduation)	Graduate Outcomes

TEF = Teaching Excellence and Student Outcomes Framework.
Source: Compiled by the author from various sources.

Design and Assessment of the Teaching Excellence and Student Outcomes Framework

The TEF was designed by the UK Department for Education, with the Higher Education Funding Council—and subsequently the Office for Students—responsible for its implementation. The government undertook a series of consultations with the sector, through the publication of Green and White papers quality (Department for Business, Innovation and Skills 2015), but final decisions rested with the minister for universities and science. This differed significantly from the standards which have tended to emerge from the sector itself—led by official sector bodies—rather than being directly introduced by the government.

The TEF (Table 3) assesses universities in three categories, with six metrics running across these, and provides awards in three levels: bronze, silver, and gold. The first category—teaching quality—assesses the extent to which students are stimulated and challenged; the second category—learning environment—the effectiveness of facilities and resources which are in place to support their learning; and the third category—student outcomes and learning gain—the extent to which they can achieve their goals, with a particular emphasis on those from disadvantaged backgrounds.

What TEF awards mean

An institution is awarded bronze for "delivering teaching, learning and outcomes for its students that meet rigorous national quality requirements for UK higher education," silver for delivering "high quality" outcomes which "consistently exceed rigorous national quality requirements," and gold for "delivering consistently outstanding teaching, learning and outcomes" which are of "the highest quality found in the UK" (Office for Students 2018).

At the highest level—gold—a university's courses are deemed to have achieved "consistently outstanding outcomes" for students, with a particular emphasis on progression to highly skilled employment and further study. The design and assessment of a university's courses are judged to provide "outstanding levels of stretch" and all students are "significantly challenged," with optimum levels of contact time. The institution is noted to provide outstanding personalized provision, which secures high levels of engagement from students; its physical and digital learning resources are outstanding and consistently used by students; and students are "consistently and frequently engaged with developments from the forefront of research, scholarship or practice." Finally, there is evidence that an institutional culture that recognizes and rewards excellence has become embedded.

Process of assessment

Each institution is assessed against a series of core and split metrics. These draw on datasets collected by the Higher Education Statistics Agency, the Office for Students, and others, and each metric is calculated using 3 years of student data. From the beginning of the TEF, these included the Graduate Outcomes survey on employment and further study 15 months after graduation (Graduate Outcomes 2020) and the National Student Survey of final year students.[11] Split metrics are used to adjust for performance within subgroups, and to consider diverse student backgrounds. The combined metrics are then contextualized—using data on the size, location, and student body of the institution—and then benchmarked—using a weighted sector average—based on the characteristics of that institution's students. This is designed to give a "hypothesis" for a university's TEF award, against which scores can be judged, and unexpected results flagged (Gunn 2018a).

The metrics used have been progressively updated, based on initial learnings and critique from within the sector, and thus it is difficult to compare awards across years. From Year 3 the National Student Survey metric was halved, low and high scores were flagged, supplementary metrics were introduced, and adjustments were made for institutions with significant numbers of part-time students. In Year 4, new metrics for the student voice were introduced, student engagement metrics were changed, and employment outcomes were reduced to one metric.

The contextualized metrics and benchmarking process are a notable feature of the TEF: they are an attempt to make it a relative rather than an absolute assessment of performance such that a university is judged against institutions with a similar intake of students. This means that a university with an intake of students from disadvantaged backgrounds, or with lower educational outcomes at 18—but which can demonstrate excellent teaching—can achieve gold, just as an institution that recruits students with the highest outcomes at 18, and which needs to make relatively lower additional investments in teaching to achieve excellent outcomes could—in theory—achieve bronze or silver.

In parallel to the assessment of institutional data, institutions are invited to submit an additional narrative explaining how their teaching and learning activities ensure high quality provision. This allows them to identify particularly distinctive practices, which may not be visible from the data. An independent panel including students and academics is then convened to judge the awards (Universities UK 2020).

TEF outcomes
The TEF process and results

The TEF has run for 4 years. The first year (TEF year 1; 2016) used QAA data to qualify universities to the TEF, and all those who qualified could increase fees in line with inflation. The TEF's first full round was in 2017 (TEF year 2), but was a voluntary exercise, with the first awards, published in June 2017 and valid until 2020 (this was later extended to 2021). Despite being voluntary, 300 institutions participated, with all except one English university and half of Scottish and Welsh universities submitting for assessment. Of the 134 institutions that took part, 33% achieved gold, 49% silver, and 18% bronze. Following the 2017 UK general election, fees were capped at £9,250 per student per year, and institutions receiving a bronze award reverted to the £9,000 floor, with others allowed to vary their fees up to the inflationary cap.

TEF year 3 took place in 2018. Thirty-one institutions assessed in 2017 reapplied in 2018, several of which were high-ranked research-intensive universities that were unhappy with their lower scores. Thirteen of the 31 improved their position, including four research intensive universities. In 2019, the latest year for which data is available, 28% of institutions that were assessed were awarded gold, 49% silver, and 22% bronze. A small number received "provisional" awards, meaning that full data was not available to assess them. The fact that the metrics have been changed in the first years of the assessment means that it is difficult to interpret the results and to

---

[11]   Until 2018, this was known as the Destination of Leavers from Higher Education (DLHE) survey.

make comparisons between awards across years. The 2020 TEF was expected to be compulsory for all English higher education institutions, but was paused due to the COVID-19 pandemic.

Subject level assessment

Because teaching quality resides primarily at the program level—rather than at the institutional level—an institution with a particular TEF award can have degree programs that vary widely in quality: a bronze institution could have silver and gold programs, and a gold institution could have bronze or silver programs. In 2017–2018 and 2018–2019, a subject level assessment was piloted to show quality at a level below the institution, and in response to the observation that quality could vary significantly within a single institution (Ashwin 2020). Two approaches were piloted: the first was top-down and by exception, in which metrics were used to see if performance at subject level differed from the institutional performance, with a full assessment then run if it did; the second was bottom-up, where all subjects were assessed, and this was used to derive the institutional level award. Because the pilots were designed to test methods, the results were not published. Fifty institutions participated in the first year of the pilot. The subject pilot was not popular and university bodies urged it be dropped (Universities UK 2019).[12]

Impact of TEF results and reactions from the sector

The TEF generated strong reactions when the first results were published in 2017 (Gunn 2018b). The results produced an "unfamiliar hierarchy of institutions" (Gunn 2018a) with a mix of older, high-ranking research universities and newer universities achieving a gold award. Several research-intensive universities rejected the results when they were awarded lower scores, and questioned the validity of the process, leading to a series of appeals (Universities UK 2017b). More than half of the Russell Group of research-intensive universities did not achieve a gold award, while institutions lower down the established league tables did substantially better (The Independent 2017).

It is difficult to know whether the TEF has achieved its fourfold aims. An independent review was commissioned, and sought evidence on how well the TEF worked, whether the ratings were right, the extent to which it had changed the educational experience of students, the value and cost-effectiveness of the TEF as an exercise, and its fairness (Universities UK 2019). The report was subsequently published in January 2021, along with a response from the UK government. The UK Office for Students is planning to develop a new framework for the TEF during 2021.[13] However, submissions to the review provide indications of how it has been received within the sector, and what can be observed of its initial impact. Further published reactions—both formal papers and reports and more informal commentaries in the HE press and on sector blogs—provide some indication of whether its methods are likely to achieve its aims.

Indications of positive impact

While it was not welcomed by some, the fact that the TEF disrupted an established hierarchy, based on the age and prestige of institutions and their position in existing rankings, is seen to be positive (Hillman 2017). One vice provost of a research-intensive university—speaking at a high-level conference—welcomed the fact that the TEF had forced such institutions to pay closer attention to teaching quality (The Times Higher Education 2017), while the TEF assessment panel chair argued that it had "shifted the dial" and "highlighted outstanding practice in previously overlooked parts of the sector" (Husbands 2019). It recognizes that many newer universities are providing a high-quality learning experience to students and investing significant resources to do so.

---

12   The results of a second pilot from 2018–2019 were published in 2021. https://www.officeforstudents.org.uk/publications/tef-findings-from-the-second-subject-level-pilot-2018-19/.

13   The report of the review was subsequently published in January 2021, along with a response from the UK government. The UK Office for Students is planning to develop a new framework for the TEF during 2021.

A review by Universities UK (UUK) —the representative body for UK universities—suggested that as a response to the TEF, its members were investing more in teaching and learning, updating strategies to engage employers, monitoring core TEF indicators, and beginning to incorporate these into institutional indicators, with an indication that teaching and learning had attained greater strategic visibility (Universities UK 2019). A report from the University and College Union (UCU–the principal trade union for academic lecturers) also noted that some changes had been observed (O'Leary et al. 2019). Changes were observed in policy related to teaching and learning, with an increase in opportunities as a result to gain recognition and promotion for teaching, rather than just research, and that there had been some small investments in research related to teaching and learning. Some changes in practice were noted, in the greater use of learning analytics, an increase in the evaluation of teaching programs, an increase in performance-management led observations, the standardization of student assessment and evaluations (and an increase in student evaluations), and the introduction of requirements for teaching staff to gain teaching qualifications.

Critical responses

Although both the UUK and UCU reports identified positive impacts, they also made several criticisms. Other commentaries from the sector have also expressed concerns with both the methods applied, the appropriateness and value of the exercise, the extent to which it provides useful evidence to the public or institutions, and its cost.

Defining teaching excellence

As several commentators have noted, teaching excellence is a difficult concept to define, being both value-laden and context specific, with no consensus in the literature (Gunn 2018a; O'Leary et al. 2019). Evidence on what drives quality in universities is largely overlooked (O'Leary et al. 2019). To measure student outcomes, the TEF relies heavily on graduate employment data. This suggests that the primary aim of universities is to provide students with the skills that their prospective employers seek, but in doing so ignores the wider purposes and value of higher education; to both individuals and society (Ashwin 2020).

Impact on teaching practices

UUK reported that while teaching had attained greater visibility in the period of the review, no institutions had initiated new programs of activity specifically to respond to the TEF, with most either reviewing protocols, accelerating existing changes, or continuing with those which had already been planned (Ashwin 2020; Universities UK 2019). UCU noted greater evidence of change in the "post-1992 institutions," created when polytechnics, teaching, and art colleges were granted university status.[14] Institutions also expressed concerns that the TEF had led them to put more effort into monitoring metrics rather than providing support to actual teaching practice, that its approach emphasizes competition rather than collaboration within the sector and leading to a more risk-averse and thus uniform set of approaches.

Value to students

It is not yet clear how students or prospective students will draw on the TEF. Because of the link between the TEF and student fees, the National Union of Students urged students to boycott the National Student Survey, meaning that this data was not available for some institutions. Although the awards themselves are simple to read with their bronze, silver, and gold labels, UUK argues that the complexity of the process, and the many metrics used, means it is difficult for students to understand and thus the clarity of the exercise for prospective students is undermined. It also suggests that metrics should be adjusted to better reflect students' experience of teaching and learning, rather than eventual graduate employment outcomes (Universities UK 2019).

---

14   Many of these institutions had historically had a stronger focus on teaching and preparation for professional practice, in addition to applied research.

A consortium of student unions commissioned research on students' views (Trendence UK 2017). Students were broadly positive about an exercise to encourage excellence in teaching, and half would have reconsidered their choice of institution if it had been awarded bronze. However, less than half favored a national framework, indicating that institutional measures were more useful. More students preferred direct feedback to teaching staff, or an end of year evaluation, for measuring excellence rather than the TEF approach. When asked which factors demonstrated a university's excellent teaching, they rated the quality of teaching and the teachers themselves as the most important factor, with graduate employment in seventh and bottom place, and student satisfaction fifth. The TEF's usefulness for serving students' informational needs has also been criticized because the data a prospective student uses could be produced 4 years before the date they finally enter university (Ashwin 2020).

Metrics

Many commentators have expressed concerns with the metrics used and the complexity of the process. UUK notes that some metrics used relied on data that was over 10 years old and that in selecting the metrics there was a greater emphasis on those which enabled differentiation between institutions rather than on the reliability of the data and the judgments made as a result (Universities UK 2019).

Although the TEF set out to measure quality, UUK argues that by drawing heavily on student satisfaction data, it does more to measure the student experience, rather than teaching quality. Ashwin notes that the TEF metrics consider teaching contact time, but that there is no evidence to suggest that this has an impact on student learning and could be "gamed" by being recorded differently. On the other hand, the expertise of teachers is proven to have an impact on student learning, but is not considered in the metrics used (Ashwin 2020).

Criticisms of the graduate outcomes metric relate to the influence that other factors have on employment and earnings, according to sectors or regions that may typically have lower rates of pay (for example, nursing and education). There is also evidence that family background significantly influences a graduate's earnings, unrelated to teaching and learning quality (Universities UK 2019).

There has been further criticism from the Royal Statistical Society of how data have been used and presented in the TEF, including the extent to which the bronze, silver, and gold ratings mask the level of uncertainty with results, the lack of comparability of awards between institutions (because of their different missions and backgrounds), and the indirect link with excellence (Royal Statistical Society 2019). Confidence in the core metrics, and the cost of gathering and processing the data, has led Universities UK to argue against the subject level approach, because it would be a significant additional cost, and would exacerbate the weaknesses already identified without any evidence that it would do more to help students make decisions (Universities UK 2019).

Academic teachers' views

The UCU commissioned a survey of its members (O'Leary et al. 2019): 6,000 members were surveyed, and a series of interviews were undertaken with officials closely involved with the TEF. The TEF was reported to be deeply unpopular, and only 1 in 10 members welcomed its introduction. Criticisms included:

(i)   It did not allow valid and reliable judgments about teaching excellence.
(ii) Assessment methods were not direct measures of teaching quality, and data could only be indirectly related to teaching practice.
(iii) It had become a marketing tool for universities.
(iv) Limited evidence that it led to the recognition of good teaching, or promotion, within universities.
(v)   Excellent teaching was treated as an individual rather than collective exercise, which was divisive and promoted unhealthy competition between teaching staff.
(vi) Increased workloads and the paperwork required meant less time was spent on teaching preparation.

Lessons

Providing lessons learned is complicated by the fact that it was—in many ways—a political as well as technocratic exercise, which was founded on a particular understanding of what universities and the teaching they provide is for. The TEF both sought to improve quality in universities and to drive and justify changes to university funding models and regulation.

Involving academics and the sector more in its development. The TEF has positively focused greater attention on teaching and learning. However, strong reactions in the sector suggest that more could have been done to involve the sector in its development.

Achieving greater consensus on what excellent teaching is. It would help such an initiative to develop a stronger consensus from the outset as to what excellent teaching is, and what is known to lead to improvements in education outcomes for students.

Recognizing the benefits of university education beyond employment and earnings. It would improve its acceptability and value within the sector if it more strongly recognized the contribution of university education to societies through the education of (predominantly) young people. For teachers whose motivation is rooted in their subjects and in a commitment to nurturing critical thinkers, the TEF does little to incentivize and recognize their efforts.

Recognizing the danger that metrics may be gamed and will not lead to investment in the right places. The fact that the TEF is seen to measure the wrong things—proxies for teaching quality, rather than teaching quality itself—mean that there is a risk that the process will be gamed; with an emphasis on investments to influence metrics, rather than to improve the teaching experience for students.

Considering the extent to which research and teaching are separated. Research and teaching are now measured by different assessment exercises. In some institutions, this has reportedly led to the separation of teaching and research posts, with academics placed on contracts, and with risks that students do not benefit from the research activities of the universities.

Developing a framework that allows for a differentiated sector and diversity within it. A critique of the current TEF is that it does not recognize and support the emergence of a diverse sector, for example, in recognizing the needs of mid-career and mature students. Metrics also need to allow for the backgrounds of students, particularly disadvantaged students.

Avoiding piecemeal changes to the metrics: While an iterative approach, piloting assessment over several phases, allowing for a live experiment, and for adjustments to be made, it also damaged confidence in the results.

Africa—Technology-Enhanced Learning Workshop for University Lecturers

Author: Fiona Khandoker, Programme Manager, The Association of Commonwealth Universities, ACU, (East Africa)

*Intervention and Results section directly copied from Partnership Impact Enhancement (IPIE) workshop report, written by Faith Malala.

Context

The Partnership for Enhanced and Blended Learning (PEBL)—an initiative funded by the Department for International Development of the United Kingdom under the Strategic Partnerships for Higher Education Innovation and Reform program—aims to address the academic staff shortages that many east African universities currently face. It enables universities to share scarce teaching resources through quality assured, credit-bearing degree courses, delivered through blended learning. It equips academics in more than 20 universities with the knowledge and skills to develop and teach blended courses. One of the many capacity development interventions implemented by the partnership was the "Technology Enhancement in Teaching and Learning Across East Africa" workshop. It was designed and delivered in collaboration with another Strategic Partnerships for Higher Education Innovation and Reform partnership titled "Pedagogical Leadership in Africa (PedaL)" and supported by the Inter-Partnership Impact Enhancement Grant of £40,000.

Background

As the Fourth Industrial Revolution becomes imminent, the use of technology as a tool for transforming teaching and learning across programs becomes even more prominent. Within this context, African universities are struggling to catch up against a backdrop of constraints such as large class sizes, small numbers of highly qualified academics, insufficient teaching and learning materials, poor infrastructure, limited research capacity, heightened expectations of stakeholders, and weak institutional quality assurance and enhancement mechanisms. Access to digital learning spaces is constrained by weak ICT capacities and weak infrastructure including limited bandwidth and unreliable connectivity, inadequate competencies of instructors, and a culture of didactic teaching.

The Fourth Industrial Revolution places new demands on the work of teachers as the driving force in a teaching and learning environment. Digital competency is becoming a prerequisite for teaching yet, many university academics have limited digital competencies. In most universities, integration of technology is consistent with a narrow view of using some form of slides or placing content on a dormant e-learning platform/Learning Management System (LMS).

The PedaL-PEBL Inter-Partnership Training on Technology Enhanced Learning workshop was designed to provide foundational pedagogical and technical knowledge and skills to teaching staff in African universities. This specific program plan was designed for blended learning delivery. The first part—the pre-workshop—was delivered asynchronously through Moodle over 4 days. The second part of the training was delivered face-to-face over 2 days in Nairobi in August 2019. Post-workshop online support was also provided over 5 days (Box 5).

Intervention

During the training, participants were introduced to the Moodle LMS, from the perspective of a student and as an instructor. From the student's perspective, the focus was on gaining practical knowledge on logging in, setting up a profile and general preferences, navigating the system, commenting on and creating discussion boards, and attaching files. From the instructor's perspective, the sessions built on knowledge on the Moodle LMS by focusing on gaining practical knowledge on self-enrollment, creating and uploading resources (files and folders), online communication (forums, discussion boards, and chats), creating assignments, quizzes, lessons, and using the grade book. The workshop was delivered through guided tutorials by a team of facilitators. Supporting material, such as written tutorials and video simulations, allowed participants to practice the skills learned in their own time.

The training aimed at achieving two key objectives:
  (i)   Enhancing the knowledge, skills, and experiences of academics in use of the Moodle;
  (ii) Unlocking intrinsic motivation of academics to innovate in integrating technology in teaching and learning;

The training also included activities that were aligned to the set objectives:
  (i)   Training faculty members in the Moodle Learning Management System; and
  (ii) Facilitating teaching staff to create a variety of innovative learning tasks to be delivered on the Learning Management System.

Box 5:   Developing an Online Course

Part One: Developing an Online Course

Introduction to Learning Management Systems

The session introduced various concepts used in TEL, such as:

- Alternative Assessments
- Authentic Assessment
- Blended learning
- E-Assessment or Online Assessment
- Innovative teaching and assessment
- Open and Distance Learning (ODL)
- Open Education Practices (OEP)
- Open Educational Resources (OER)
- Technology Enhanced Learning

The participants were then introduced to the concept of a learning management system, advantages, challenges, and opportunities availed by using LMS. Most participants were interested in gaining proficiency in using an LMS they noted that while LMS existed in their institutions, they were not fully utilized due to a capacity gap. Furthermore, some reported that they are expected to design online courses without any capacity and skills building on how to do it. Most of these efforts have been frustrated mostly due to lack of capacity building and planning, rather than due to negative attitudes toward use of technology in learning.

It was noted that most institutions have LMS that are not fully explored due to challenges such as lack of proper infrastructure. Some universities do not have stable internet or even university information and communication technology support staff. Some classes even lack mere functional power sockets. Some of the participants had no idea of what an LMS is since some universities encourage optional LMS use. Despite these challenges, it was affirmed that the integration of technology in teaching and learning should be a constant song in the institutions.

Using Moodle to Facilitate Learning

This session was concerned with using LMS to facilitate learning through various forms such as:

- Discussion forums
- Using messaging within the LMS
- Uploading course content
- Developing assignment and quiz activities
- Using the gradebook

Each participant developed their individual online course on the LMS with each of these activities.

Part Two: Grading Using an LMS

The session was concerned with grading online engagements including forums, assignments and quizzes using a learning management system. The tasks involved:

- Setting up a gradebook
- Creating categories

continued on next page

Box 5   *continued*

- Configuring aggregation methods for the gradebook categories
- Configuring forums and assignments for grading
- Weighting of assignments, forums, and categories in the gradebook
- Setting up a rubric
- Using feedback files
- Using offline grading worksheet

Participants were divided into small groups. Each participant enrolled other participants in the groups as student users. The role play involved the users engaging in gradable activities in their courses created by their colleagues. At the end of the exercise, each participant graded the following activities:

- Rating a forum
- Using a rubric to grade
- Using an offline grading worksheet to grade assignments

LMS = Learning Management System, TEL = Technology Enhanced Learning.
Source: Compiled by author.

One of the participants advised that they only had a theoretical idea of grading and that the training made it easier for them to put it into practice. They found the grading exercise challenging, but helpful. It was evident that many participants were significantly unfamiliar with grading using LMS. After the role plays and class activities on the same, many were confident and ready to use it.

After the training, the participants registered feedback: 100% expressed that they were satisfied with the training. They described themselves as "transformed," "better," "revived," and "changed." In addition to the above, 72% of the participants left the training ready to be ambassadors in their various institutions feeling equipped to support other faculty members and students in integrating technology into teaching and learning. Thirdly, 95% of the participants alluded that they would confidently recommend technology-enhanced learning to their colleagues.

Results

PEBL aimed to ensure that enough lecturers were trained to teach the newly developed blended courses. This aim was materialized as academics from more than 12 institutions collaborated with management in their respective universities to pilot blended learning as a mode of delivery. Between September 2019 and March 2020, more than 1,500 students—from universities that participated in the training—used blended courses. According to survey results, more than 80% of respondents were satisfied with the new form of delivery.

The intervention also served as a cascade training program. Those academics trained through the workshop went back to their respective institutions and passed on the training to their peers. More than 200 additional lecturers were trained in this way in more than five universities in Kenya, Tanzania, and Uganda.

Lessons

One of the most important learnings was that such training was highly needed. Institutions must prioritize capacity development so that academics are motivated to use technological tools in teaching. It will not be enough for universities to create policies around technology enhanced learning. Resources must be dedicated to training large numbers of staff.

The structure of the training needs to be modified so that more teachers are trained from each institution so that they can collectively organize training sessions for their peers in their respective institutions and pass on the knowledge.

One of the most important learnings was that such training is necessary and will need to be scaled-up across countries with a rapidly increasing student population.

If institutions from various countries in the same region come together to exchange knowledge and expertise, they can elevate their skills more effectively. Moreover, they can get in touch with each other whenever they face challenges. Being in similar contexts helps because it allows academics to have a deeper understanding of the issues at hand and provides insights and solutions.

Recommendations

The case studies described in this paper reflect the core aspects of successful teacher training systems: well-structured pre- and in-service training components, adequate and targeted pedagogical and domain-specific training components, and innovative practices in teaching and learning methods. A holistic approach in reforming teacher training is needed, which aims at ensuring interconnectivity between pre- and in-service training and the integration of pedagogical and domain-specific training components. Moving away from ad hoc, short-term training courses for teachers, the focus needs to be on supporting sustainable systems for high-quality, relevant pre- and in-service training for teachers.

Recommendations for K-12

All five K-12 teacher education case studies in this publication give out a clear message: teacher pre-service and in-service should be developed holistically and with a long perspective. More detailed recommendations are given to K-12 education below.

Teacher education **should be developed as a whole**, and not be based on projects, but be systematic and ongoing. Teachers should be able to gain higher academic degrees—that is bachelor's or even master's degrees—and teacher education should always be given in a university. **Policies and incentives supporting the capacity development of teachers need to be in place** to create a framework that defines the regulations, structure, and resources for a successful teacher education system. In future ADB education projects, a strong emphasis should be given on academic teacher pre-service education and its development in the national context.

Due to the low quality of pre-service teacher training and education, teachers also have weak pedagogical and subject knowledge. This is also related to the low quality of teacher-trainers. In coming ADB projects, **emphasis should be placed on choosing and training the best persons to become teacher trainers and educators**. They should have a very wide teaching experience, deep subject knowledge, and the latest experience on pedagogical trends.

Teachers should be systematically supported during their careers from all levels of the education administration, that is head teachers in the school, but also district, regional, and national managers. In-service teacher training should also be ongoing. All ADB teacher in-service programs should include a systemic way to advance their skills, including in assessment and administration, as well as pedagogical and subject knowledge. Teachers should be able to grow individually in their profession and in that way become better educators.

Strong institutional leadership is crucial for teachers' continuous capacity development as a clear vision and mission. The autonomy of faculties and the learning environment will enable teachers to continuously upgrade their skills and make use of their better competencies. The training of school management and ensuring that trained leaders and teachers are given the financial means, infrastructure, and equipment to implement what they have been trained to do will ensure the sustainability of teacher training.

Recommendations for TVET

In the TVET sector, teachers play a key role in equipping students with skills that meet the needs of the labor market. Case studies from Singapore, Viet Nam, and Ethiopia demonstrate key elements and preconditions for pre-service and in-service TVET teacher training.

The integration of pedagogy and domain-specific elements is highly relevant for TVET teacher training. The transformation of a traditional TVET model—which separates practical training from theory to a holistic model that integrates both technical knowledge and practical skills—requires a domain-specific pedagogy approach. TVET teachers need to be prepared to deliver training in an authentic learning environment that reflects workplace settings and includes the latest technologies. To ensure the adoption of demand-oriented and work-based teaching and learning, a domain-specific pedagogy approach in TVET teacher training is needed.

Industry exposure during pre- and in-service training is a key factor for obtaining relevant, up-to-date experience and skills. Continuous opportunities for industry exposure—such as through joint projects—will create an in-depth understanding of the future workplaces of their students which will help TVET teachers to design and implement training that is linked more closely to the needs of industry. Attracting people with previous industry experience to become TVET teachers and promoting the recruitment of part-time or temporary teachers from industry are further intervention areas that contribute to the increased relevance of TVET.

Industry partnerships allow TVET teacher training institutes to improve synergies with companies for teacher professional development by aligning TVET teacher training closely with the needs of industry. Supporting policies and incentives—such as tax incentives—will facilitate TVET-industry linkages. Industry involvement in the development of TVET teacher training programs and the delivery of training ensures that teachers obtain relevant skills and up-to-date knowledge of the labor market requirements. Building the capacity of TVET teachers and managers to initiate and maintain industry linkages—such as for student apprenticeships— remains one of the core elements of a demand-oriented training system.

Selected institutions function as hubs or centers of excellence for TVET teacher training providing not only relevant pedagogical and domain-specific theoretical and practical pre- and in-service training, but also training for TVET teachers and managers on topics including industry linkages, technology use, curriculum, and learning materials development. Furthermore, TVET research on new models for TVET, vocational pedagogy, teaching and learning outcomes, industry collaboration, and others conducted by the centers of excellence contributes to the reform of the overall TVET system. To ensure the relevance and demand-orientation of training and services offered by centers of excellence, the involvement of industry in the establishment and development of these centers of excellence is crucial.

Continuous capacity development opportunities and framework conditions for sustaining results need to be in place. Strong institutional leadership is crucial for ensuring continuous learning opportunities for TVET teachers and the utilization of their improved competencies. Coaching and mentoring by experienced master trainers or regular exchange with peers ensures the successful implementation of the gained skills in the daily teaching practice. Resources—including a budget for consumables, training infrastructure, and equipment—are important aspects for implementing and sustaining results of TVET teacher training.

Policies and incentives for TVET teacher professional and career development are important conditions for high-quality TVET. A framework that covers regulations on integrated pre- and in-service training, requirements on industry experience or exposure, policies on recruitment, selection, career development, and salary structure, and that also considers requirements for inclusive education will be the basis for creating and sustaining high-quality, demand-oriented training through competent, motivated, and innovative TVET teachers.

Recommendations for Higher Education

Even though the recognition of the importance of education capacity of universities is essential, the strategies to improve pedagogical practices and strengthen the quality of education in higher education can be different depending on the country situation. Policy intervention patterns have been used by various countries such as the US (which is strengthening its teaching capacity by university autonomy), the UK (which defines teachers' competency at the national level and establishes a systematic capacity building system), and ROK (which is inducing university efforts through university evaluation certification and financial support projects to strengthen their educational competency).

Establishing a specialized center supporting teaching in a university is recommended. Many countries establish a center and organize various activities to improve the quality of teaching. The mission of these centers has been expanded to support students who have struggled in study and research. CTLs can run various activities including improving teaching capacity, lectures for teaching methodology, professor community support, counseling for teaching, and research for improving teaching methods. In the COVID-19 situation, training programs for blended learning and online learning have been most needed between professors.

Government intervention is recommended to improve teaching quality universities. Some economies make a separate assessment system to evaluate universities' intention and effort to teach well, and others include universities' effort to teach well in the general accreditation index and provide financial support to the activities of universities' effort. The third approach is universities' autonomous investment and effort to improve the teaching quality, like in Hong Kong, China. It is recommended that the most applicable and effective approach and support is provided to the economy for each method.

University Community activities can be encouraged. It is necessary to support the mutual sharing of best practices by organizing and operating a network of departments to strengthen university educational competency through the collaboration among universities.

Professors should be evaluated on educational capability as well as performance achievement. For a university to improve the quality of education offered by individual professors and teachers, consideration should be given not only to research performance and promotion evaluations, but also to educational competency, student employment rates, and cooperation with industry. If efforts to introduce and guide various teaching methods are not reflected in performance evaluations, increasing the participation of existing teachers will have limitations, except for new teachers.

The goal of this report is to illuminate the features of professional development that are effective in hopes that these cases can help inform policy makers and practitioners of productive suggestions for teacher professional development. By sharing successful cases and lessons learned and recommendations, policy makers and practitioners can explore what went well, what could be improved, and how lessons could be incorporated into their programs.

Within its Strategy 2030's first operational priority, ADB will scale-up teacher and trainer professional development. Learning from international best practices and its project preparation and implementation experience, ADB will expand its focus to follow strategic elements in the professional development of teachers.

References

AdvanceHE. 2011. *UK Professional Standards Framework* (UKPSF). https://www.advance-he.ac.uk/guidance/teaching-and-learning/ukpsf.

AdvanceHE. 2020. *AdvanceHE Development Pathway.* https://www.advance-he.ac.uk/programmes-events/development-programmes/advance-he-development-pathway.

K. Akyeampong. 2003. *Teacher Training in Ghana- Does it Count? Multi-Site Teacher Education Research Project (MUSTER). Country Report 1.* DFID.

K. Ananiadou and M. Claro. 2009. *21st century skills and competences for new millennium learners in OECD countries.* Paris: OECD Publishing.

P. Ashwin. 2020. *Knowledge Is Power: The Purpose of Quality Teaching.* Wonkhe (blog). 10 February. https://wonkhe.com/blogs/knowledge-is-power-the-purpose-of-quality-teaching/.

P. Ashwin. n.d. *Making Sense of the Teaching Excellence Framework (TEF) Results, 2.*

ADB. 2019. *Indonesia: Supporting the Advanced Knowledge and Skills for Sustainable Growth Project.* Manila.

———. 2012. *Papua New Guinea: Critical Development Constraints.* Manila.

———. 2011. *Improving Instructional Quality Focus on Faculty Development.* Manila.

Australian Council for Educational Research (ACER). 2019. *Papua New Guinea Pacific Islands Literacy and Numeracy Assessment (PILNA) 2018 Results.* Suva.

D.L. Ball and D.K. Cohen. 1999. *Developing practices, developing practitioners: Toward a practice-based theory of professional education.* In L. Darling-Hammond and G. Sykes, eds. Teaching as the learning profession: Handbook of policy and practice. San Francisco, CA: Jossey-Bass.

A. Bautista and R. Ortega-Ruiz. 2015. *Teacher professional development: International perspectives and approaches.* Psychology, Society and Education. (7): pp. 343–355.

M. Barber and M. Mourshed. 2007. *How the world's best-performing school system come out on top.* New York: McKinsey & Company.

M. Binkley et al. 2012. *Defining 21st century skills.* In P. Griffin, E. Care, and B. McGaw, eds. *Assessment and teaching of 21st century skills.* Dordrecht: The Netherlands: Springer.

A.S. Bin Tariq [Interview]. 2020. *Interview: Centre of Excellence in Teaching and Learning*, Rajshahi University. Skype, 23 January.

S. Blömeke, J. Gustafsson, and R. Shavelson. 2015. *Beyond dichotomies: Competence viewed as a continuum.* Zeitschrift für Psychologie, 223, 3–13.

S. Blömeke. 2017. *Modelling teachers' professional competence as a multi-dimensional construct.* In S. Guerriero, ed., Pedagogical knowledge and the changing nature of the teaching profession. pp. 119–135. Paris: OECD Publishing.

R. Boelens, M. Voet, and B. De Wever. 2018. *The Design of Blended Learning in Response to Student Diversity in Higher Education: Instructors' Views and Use of Differentiated Instruction in Blended Learning.* Computers and Education. 120. pp. 197–212. doi: 10.1016/j.compedu.2018.02.009.

T. Booth. 2019. *Breaking Down the Barrier: Index of Inclusion.* Bristol BS4 1DQ, UK: Centre for Studies on Inclusive Education (CSIE). http://www.csie.org.uk/resources/inclusion-index-explained.shtml.

British Council, Bangladesh. 2015. *Centre of Excellence in Teaching and Learning (CETL).* https://www.britishcouncil.org.bd/en/programmes/education/higher/centre-excellence-teaching-learning.

T. Buchanan, P. Sainter, and G. Saunders. 2013. *Factors Affecting Faculty Use of Learning Technologies: Implications for Models of Technology Adoption.* Journal of Computing in Higher Education. 25(1). pp. 1–11.

Busan National University Centre for Teaching and Learning. 2019. *Annual Report 2018.*

F. Caena. 2017. *Weaving the fabric: Teaching and teacher education ecosystems.* In B. Hudson, ed. Overcoming fragmentation in teacher education policy and practice. Cambridge, UK: Cambridge University Press.

F. Caena and C. Redecker. 2019. *Aligning teacher competence frameworks to 21st century challenges: The case for the European digital competence framework for educators.* Educ. 2019. 54: pp. 356–369. https ://doi.org/10.1111/ejed.12345.

Cambridge Education, United Kingdom. 2014. *Girls Participatory Approaches for Student Success G-PASS Programme in Ghana- Technical Proposal.*

Centre of Excellence in Teaching and Learning. n. d. *Guidelines for Peer Observation.* Bangladesh: Khuna University.

C.R. Clotfelter, H.F. Ladd, and J.L. Vigdor. 2006. *Teacher-student matching and the assessment of teacher effectiveness.* Journal of Human Resources. 41(4): pp. 778–820.

Council of Europe. 2001. *Common European Framework of Reference for Languages: Learning, Teaching, Assessment, (CEFR): The CEFR Companion Volume with New Descriptors, 2018.* France: Strasbourg Cedex. https://rm.coe.int/cefr-companion-volume-with-new-descriptors-2018/1680787989.

V.M. Crecci and D. Fiorentini. 2018. *Professional development within teacher learning communities.* Educação em Revista. Vol. 34. https://www.scielo.br/scielo.php?pid=S0102-46982018000100111&script=sci_arttext&tlng=en.

L. Darling-Hammond, R. Chung Wei, and A. Andree. 2010. *How high-achieving countries develop great teachers.* Stanford Center for Opportunity Policy in Education Research Brief. pp. 1–8.

L. Darling-Hammond, M.E. Hyler, and M. Garder. 2017. *Effective Teacher Professional Development.* Palo Alto, CA: Learning Policy Institute.

Department for Business, Innovation and Skills, United Kingdom. 2015. *Fulfilling Our Potential: Teaching Excellence, Social Mobility and Student Choice.* London.

———. 2016a. *Higher Education and Research Bill: Factsheet.* London.

———. 2016b. *Summary of Responses: Fulfilling Our Potential: Teaching Excellence, Social Mobility and Student Choice.* London.

Department of Education, Philippines. 2020. *Vision, Mission, Core Values and Mandate.* Pasig City: Department of Education.

———. 2019. Number of Teachers in Public ES, JHS and SHS: SY2018–2019. *Basic Education Information System.* Pasig City: Department of Education.

———. 2016. *The Learning Action Cell as a K to 12 Basic Education Program School-Based Continuing Professional Development Strategy for the Improvement of Teaching and Learning.* DO 35, S. 2016.

———. 2015. *Guidelines on the Early Language Literacy and Numeracy Program— Professional Development Component.* DO 12, S. 2015.

———. 2011. *Policies and Guidelines on the Implementation of the Universal Kindergarten Education for SY 2011–2012.* DO 37, S. 2011.

Department of Education, Region VI: Western Visayas, Philippines. 2019. *National Orientation on the Adoption of the Blended Delivery Model for TPD Rollout of the ELLN Digital for K to 3 Teachers.* RA No. 86, S. 2019.

Department for Education, United Kingdom. 2017. *Teaching Excellence and Student Outcomes Framework Specification.* London.

———. 2019. *Independent Review of the Teaching Excellence and Student Outcomes Framework (TEF): Call for Views.* London.

Department for International Development (DFID), United Kingdom. 2012. *Girls Unite and Pass (Participatory Approaches for Student Success) Business Case.*

J. Dickinson. 2019. *There's Tension in this TEF Review.* Wonkhe (blog). 5 November.

Divine Word University and VSO PNG. 2012. *Capacity Needs Analysis and Capacity Development Plan for the PNG National Education System, Key Deliverable 3: Capacity Needs Analysis.* Port Moresby.

Education International. 2011. *Quality Educators: An International Study of Teacher Competences and Standards.* Education International. Brussels.

Education Management Information System (EMIS). 2016. *Education Statistics*. National Department of Education Statistical Division. Port Moresby.

Education Quality Assessment Program (EQAP). 2016. *Pacific Benchmarking for Education Results—Synthesis Report: Papua New Guinea, Samoa, and Solomon Islands*. Suva, Fiji.

European Commission. 2013. *Supporting teacher competence development: For better learning outcomes*. http://ec.europa.eu/education/school-education/teacher-cluster_en.htm.

European Commission for Democracy through Law (Venice Commission). 2019. *Opinion on the Law on Supporting the Functioning of the Ukrainian Language as the State Language*. Council of Europe. Venice.

European Council. 2018. *Council Recommendation of 22 May 2018 on Key Competences for Lifelong Learning. 2018/C 189/01*. European Council. Brussels.

A. Ferrari, Y. Punie, and C. Redecker. 2012. *Understanding Digital Competence in the 21st Century: An Analysis of Current Frameworks*. 21st Century Learning for 21st Century Skills. pp. 79–92.

Foundation for Information Technology Education and Development. 2017. *Annex 3: Questionnaire for ELLN Training Participants*. In Technology-Supported Teacher Professional Development in Early Literacy for K-3 Teachers: Final Performance Report 1, 1 August 2015–30 September 2017. Quezon City, Philippines.

E. Garcia and E. Weiss. 2019. *The role of early career supports, continuous professional development, and learning communities in the teacher shortage*. The fifth report in *The perfect storm in the teacher labor market* series. Washington, DC: Economic Policy Institute.

Global Partnership for Education. 2019. *A knowledge and Innovation Exchange (KIX) Discussion Paper*. Global Washington, DC: Partnership for Education.

Global Partnership for Education (GPE). 2018. *Education Sector Plan Implementation Grant & Multiplier: Boosting Education Standards Together in PNG (BEST PNG) Program*. PNG.

Government of the People's Republic of Bangladesh. 2015. *Seventh Five-Year Plan, FY2016–FY2020: Accelerating Growth, Empowering Citizens*. General Economics Division, Planning Commission. Dhaka.

Government of the Republic of the Philippines. 2013. Republic Act No. 10533. *Official Gazette*. 15 May.

———. 2016. *Republic Act No. 10912, An Act Mandating and Strengthening the Continuing Professional Development Program for All Regulated Professions, Creating the Continuing Professional Development Council, and Appropriating Funds Therefor, and For Other Related Purposes*. 3rd Regular Session, 16th Congress.

Government of the United Kingdom. 2020. *Teaching Excellence Framework: Independent Review*. February. London.

Government of Viet Nam, Directorate of Vocational Education and Training and National Institute for Vocational Training. 2019. *Vietnam Vocational Education and Training Report 2017*. Ha Noi.

———. 2018. *Vietnam Vocational Education and Training Report 2016*. Ha Noi.

Government of Viet Nam, General Statistics Office. 2018. *Statistical Yearbook of Vietnam 2018*.

———. 2018. *Report on Labour force survey 2018.* Available at https://www.gso.gov.vn/en/homepage/.

Government of Viet Nam, Ministry of Labour–Invalids and Social Affairs (MOLISA). 2017. *Circular 06/2017/ TT-BLDTBXH: Regulation on recruitment, employment and further training of VET teachers.*

——— . 2017. *Circular 15/2017/TT-BLDTBXH: Regulations on standards and criteria for accreditation of VET.*

———. 2017. *Circular 08/2017/TT-BLĐTBXH: Regulations on standards for VET teacher professional qualifications and competence.*

Government of Viet Nam, National Assembly. 2019. *Law 45/2019/QH14: Labour Code 45/2019/QH14.*

———. 2014. *Vocational Education and Training Law – Chapter V, Article 55.*

Graduate Outcomes. 2020. 21 February. Available at https://www.graduateoutcomes.ac.uk/.

C.R. Graham, W. Woodfield, and J.B. Harrison. 2013. *A Framework for Institutional Adoption and Implementation of Blended Learning in Higher Education.* The Internet and Higher Education. 18. pp. 4–14.

J. Gregory and G. Salmon. 2013. *Professional development for online university teaching.* Distance Education, *34(3).* pp. 256–270.

P. E. Griffin, E. Care, and B. McGaw, eds. 2012. *Assessment and teaching of 21st century skills.* Dordrecht, The Netherlands: Springer.

P. E. Griffin and E. Care. 2014. *Developing learners' collaborative problem solving skills (European SchoolNet Academy KeyCoNet paper). http://vp-learn ingdi aries.weebly.com/uploa ds/9/4/9/8/94981 70/developing_learners_ collaborat ve_problem_solving_p_griff in.pdf.* Accessed 3 Oct 2020.

S. Guerriero, ed. 2017. *Pedagogical knowledge and the changing nature of the teaching profession.* Paris: OECD Publishing. http://dx.doi.org/10.1787/9789264270695-en.

A. Gunn. 2018a. *Metrics and Methodologies for Measuring Teaching Quality in Higher Education: Developing the Teaching Excellence Framework (TEF).* Educational Review 70. 2 (15 March). pp. 129–148.

A. Gunn. 2018b. The UK Teaching Excellence Framework (TEF): *The Development of a New Transparency Tool.* In Adrian Curaj, Ligia Deca, and Remus Pricopie, eds. *European Higher Education Area: The Impact of Past and Future Policies.* Cham: Springer International Publishing.

T.R. Guskey. 2000. *Evaluating Professional Development.* Corwin Press. Thousand Oaks.

T.R. Guskey. 2003. *Analyzing lists of the characteristics of effective professional development to promote visionary leadership.* NASSP Bulletin, 87(637). pp. 4–20.

M. Hayden. 2019. *Challenges to higher education in Laos and Cambodia. School of Education, Southern Cross University.* Accessed 5 Oct 2020.

E.A. Hanushek and S.G. Rivkin. 2006. *Teacher quality.* In E. A. Hanushek and F. Welch. Eds., Handbook of the Economics of Education. Vol. 2. pp. 1,051–1,078. North Holland. New York, NY.

R.H. Heck. 2009. *Teacher effectiveness and student achievement: Investigating a multilevel cross-classified model.* Journal of Educational Administration. 47(2): pp. 227–249.

H. Heikkilä and L. Seppänen. 2014. *Examining Developmental Dialogue: The Emergence of Transformative Agency.* Outlines–Critical Practice Studies. 15(2). pp. 5–30.

J.H. Herman. 2012. *Faculty development programs: The frequency and variety of professional development programs available to online instructors.* Journal of Asynchronous Learning Networks. 16(5): pp. 87–102.

N. Hillman. 2017. *HEPI Director Responds to the Teaching Excellence Framework Results.* Oxford: Higher Education Policy Institute (HEPI).

Higher Education Academy. 2020. *Accreditation Aligning Professional Development to the UKPSF.* United Kingdom: Teaching and Learning Accreditation.

C. Husbands. 2019. *2019 TEF Results: Three Years of Seeking Out Excellence.* Wonkhe (blog).

International Labour Organization. 2016. *Compilation of assessment studies on technical and vocational education and training (TVET): Lao People's Democratic Republic, Mongolia, the Philippines, Thailand and Vietnam.*

JAMK. 2020. Ethiopia.

C. Johnston et al. 2019. *RISE Midline Report.* Save the Children. Port Moresby.

A. Kajamaa. 2015. *Collaborative Work Development as a Resource for Innovation and Quality Improvement in Health Care: An Example from a Hospital Surgery.* In S. Gurtner and K. Soyez, eds. Challenges and Opportunities in Health Care Management. Cham: Springer International Publishing.

G.D. Kennedy et al. 2011. *Understanding the Reasons Academics Use–and Don't Use–Endorsed and Unendorsed Learning Technologies.* ASCILITE 2011—The Australasian Society for Computers in Learning in Tertiary Education.

M. Kim. 2018. *Policy Diagnosis and strategies for higher education innovation 2 – focusing on the faculty development,* Korean Education Development Institute.

Korean Association of Centers for Teaching and Learning. 2011. *2011 University Education Development History.*

A. Kukari. 2018. *A Situation Analysis of Education in Papua New Guinea.* National Department of Education, Papua New Guinea. Port Moresby.

H.F. Ladd and L.C. Sorenson. 2017. *Returns to Teacher Experience: Student Achievement and Motivation in Middle School.* Education Finance and Policy. 12(2): pp. 241–279.

T.J.Lasley II, D. Siedentop, and R. Yinger. 2006. *A systematic approach to enhancing teacher quality: The Ohio model.* Journal of Teacher Education. 57: pp. 13–21.

D. Laurillard. 2005. E-Learning in Higher Education. In P. Ashwin, ed. *Changing Higher Education: The Development of Learning and Teaching.* London: Routledge.

M.L. Louws et al. 2017. *Teachers' professional learning goals in relation to teaching experience.* European Journal of Teacher Education. 40(4): pp. 487–504.

K. Luneta. 2011. *Initial teachers education in Southern Africa: Mentorship and teaching practicum supervision.* LAP LAMBERT Academic Publishing GmbH and Co. KG. Saarbrucken.

K. Luneta. 2012. *Designing continuous professional development programmes for teachers: A literature review.* Africa Education Review. 9(2). pp. 360-379.

K. Macdonald and B.T. Vul. 2018. *A Randomized Evaluation of a Low-Cost and Highly Scripted Teaching Method to Improve Basic Early Grade Reading in Papua New Guinea.* Policy Research Working Paper 8427. World Bank Group Education Global Practice.

J. Macdonald and A. Campbell. 2012. *Demonstrating Online Teaching in the Disciplines. A Systematic Approach to Activity Design for Online Synchronous Tuition.* British Journal of Educational Technology. 43(6). pp. 883–891.

M. Mäkinen, A. Yekunoamlak, and A. Azmera. 2019. *Towards Inclusive Education in Vocational Education: - Development Project As a Change Agent.* Ammattikasvatuksen Aikakauskirja 21 (3). pp. 35-45. https://journal.fi/akakk/article/view/87500.

A.Y. Malle. 2017. *Policy–Practice Gap in Participation of Students with Disabilities in Ethiopia's Formal Vocational Education Programme.* Doctoral dissertation. Jyväskylä Studies in Education, Psychology and Social Research. p. 578. University of Jyväskylä, Jyväskylä.

L. Manasia, M.G. Ianos, and T.D. Chicioreanu. 2020. *Pre-service teacher preparedness for fostering education for sustainable development: An empirical analysis of central dimensions of teaching readiness.* Sustainability. 12(1): p. 166.

R.L. Metsapelto et al. 2020. *Conceptual framework of teaching quality: A multidimensional adapted process model of teaching.* OVET Project Working Paper.

K.A. Meyer. 2014. *An Analysis of the Research on Faculty Development for Online Teaching and Identification of New Directions.* Journal of Asynchronous Learning Networks. 17(4). pp. 93–112.

K.W. Miller and D.M. Davidson. 2006. *What makes a secondary school science and/or mathematics teacher "highly qualified"?* Science Educator. 15(1): pp. 56–59.

Ministry of Education, Ethiopia. 1995. *Constitution of the Federal Democratic Republic of Ethiopia.*

Ministry of Education, Youth and Sport. 2015. *Teacher Policy Action Plan.* Teacher Training Department, Ministry of Education, Youth and Sport. Phnom Pehn.

L. Moghtadaie and M.Taji. 2018. *Explaining the requirement for teacher's development based on professional competencies approach.* Educational Research and Reviews. 13(14). pp. 564-569.

P.C. Moskal, C. Dziuban, and J. Hartman. 2013. *Blended Learning: A Dangerous Idea?* The Internet and Higher Education. 18. pp. 15–23.

A. Mulkeen, W. Ratteree, and I. Voss-Lengnik. 2017. *Teachers and Teacher Policy in Primary and Secondary Education.* Discussion Paper Education. Bonn: Deutsche Gesellschaft für Internationale Zusammenarbeit (GIZ) GmbH.

A. Murray. 2010. *Empowering teachers through professional development.* English Teaching Forum, 1. pp. 1-10.

P. Musset. 2010. *Initial Teacher Education and Continuing Training Policies in a Comparative Perspective: Current Practices in OECD Countries and a Literature Review on Potential Effects.* OECD Education Working Papers, No. 48. OECD Publishing.

N.P. Napier, S. Dekhane, and S. Smith. 2011. *Transitioning to Blended Learning: Understanding Student and Faculty Perceptions.* Journal of Asynchronous Learning Networks. 15(1). pp. 20–32.

National Audit Office, United Kingdom. 2017. *The Higher Education Market.* HC 629 (2017–2019). National Audit Office. London.

National Department of Education (NDOE). 2016. *National Education Plan Quality Learning for All, 2015–2019.* Papua New Guinea. Port Moresby.

————. 2018. *Education Sector Plan Implementation Grant & Multiplier: Boosting Education Standards Together in PNG (BEST PNG) Program.* Port Moresby: Papua New Guinea.

National Statistical Office (NSO), Papua New Guinea. 2011. *National Population and Housing Census 2011: Final Figures Booklet.*

M. Njenga. 2019. *Policies for Effective TVET Teacher Continuing Professional Development in Kenya.* Paper presented at 4th Carpathian Basin Educational Conference.

C.T. Nguyen. 2003. *Training High Qualified Teachers in Vietnam: Challenges and Policy Issues.*

G. Oakley, R. King, and G. Scarparolo. 2018. *An Evaluation of ELLN Digital: Technology-supported Teacher Professional Development on Early Language, Literacy and Numeracy for K-3 Teachers.* Philippines: Foundation for Information Technology Education and Development. Quezon City.

M. O'Leary, V. Cui, and A. French. 2019. *Understanding, Recognising and Rewarding Teaching Quality in Higher Education: An Exploration of the Impact and Implications of the Teaching Excellence Framework.* London: University and College Union.

Organisation for Economic Co-operation and Development (OECD). 2005. *Teachers Matter–Attracting, Developing and Retaining Effective Teachers.* Paris: OECD Publishing.

OECD.org (n.d.). *TALIS: The OECD Teaching and Learning International Survey. TALIS FAQ.* https://www.oecd.org/education/talis/talisfaq/. Accessed 4 September 2020.

Office for Students. 2018. *What Is the Teaching Excellence and Student Outcomes Framework (TEF)?—Office for Students.* United Kingdom.

P.B. PaBER. 2016. *Sythesis Report: Papua New Guinea, Somoa, Solomon Islands.* Education Quality Assessment Program (EQA). Suva, Fiji.

J. Papay and M. Kraft. 2015. *Productivity returns to experience in the teacher labor market: Methodological challenges and new evidence on long-term career improvement.* Journal of Public Economics. 130: pp. 105–119.

Papova et al. 2019. *Teacher Professional Development around the World: The Gap between Evidence and Practice.* London: Centre for Global Development.

A. Parvin. n. d. *Challenges of Quality Assurance in Teaching–Learning: Reflections on CETL-Khulna University Experience.*

_____. 2019. *Leadership and Management in Quality Assurance: Insights from the Context of Khulna University, Bangladesh.* Higher Education 77. 4 (April). pp. 739–756.

_____. 2020. [Interview]. *Interview: Centre of Excellence in Teaching and Learning,* Khulna University. Zoom, 24 April.

W.W. Porter and C.R. Graham. 2016. *Institutional Drivers and Barriers to Faculty Adoption of Blended Learning in Higher Education.* British Journal of Educational Technology. 47(4). pp. 748–762.

J. Qi. 2012. *The role of Chinese normal universities in the professional development of teachers.* A thesis submitted for the Ph.D. University of Toronto.

T. Rahman et al. 2019. *Bangladesh Tertiary Education Sector Review: Skills and Innovation for Growth.* Education Sector Review. Washington, DC: World Bank.

A.B. Ahasan Raqib. 2019. *Innovations in Teacher Training at Higher Education in Bangladesh.* Social Science Review [The Dhaka University Studies, Part-D]. 36(1).

J.K. Rice. 2003. *Teacher Quality: Understanding the Effectiveness of Teacher Attributes.* Washington DC: Economic Policy Institute.

Royal Statistical Society. 2019. *Submission to the Independent Review of the TEF.* United Kingdom.

SEA-TCF. 2018. *Southeast Asia Teachers Competency Framework (SEA-TCF).* Bangkok, Thailand: Teachers Council of Thailand.

SEAMEO INNOTECH. 2010. *Teaching Competence Standards in Southeast Asian Countries.* Philippines: SEAMEO INNOTECH.

K. Selvi. 2010. *Teachers' Competencies.* Cultra International Journal of Philosophy of Culture and Axiology. (7): pp. 167–175. 10.5840/cultura20107133.

L.S. Shulman. 2005. *Signature pedagogies in the professions.* Daedalus, *134*(3). pp. 52-59.

K. Simoncini, K. Namit, and H. Smith. 2019. *T4E Midline Report.* Port Moresby: World Vision.

Skill. n.d. *Merriam-Webster Open Dictionary.* http://www.merriamwebster.com/dictionary/skill.

H. Smith and K. Simoncini. 2018. *Literacy, Numeracy and School Survey: Baseline Report.* World Vision International in Papua New Guinea. Port Moresby.

The State Committee of Statistics. Ukraine.

Success as a Knowledge Economy: Teaching Excellence, Social Mobility and Student Choice. 2016. United Kingdom

Sumaryanta et al. 2018. *Assessing Teacher Competence and Its Follow-up to Support Professional Development Sustainability*. Journal of Teacher Education for Sustainability. 20(1). pp. 106–123.

TECIP Project in Ethiopia. 2020. Ethiopia.

The Independent. 2017. *Elite Universities Found to Have Second-Rate Teaching*. 21 June.

The Philippine Star. 2019. *Teachers' salary way below ASEAN average*. 6 July.

TPD@Scale Coalition for the Global South. 2019. *Early Language Literacy, and Numeracy (ELLN) Digital*.

Times Higher Education (THE). 2017a. *Imperial Vice-Provost: TEF a "Godsend" for University Teaching*. 1 July.

———. 2017b. TEF 2017: *"Meaningless" Results "Devoid of Credibility,"* Says v-c. 22 June.

T. Tirussew et al. 2018. *Ethiopian Education Development Roadmap (2018–2030). An Integrated Executive Summary*. Ministry of Education, Education Strategy Center. Addis Ababa.

G. Torrisi-Steele and S. Drew. 2013. *The Literature Landscape of Blended Learning in Higher Education: The Need for Better Understanding of Academic Blended Practice*. International Journal for Academic Development. 18(4). pp. 371–383.

Training of Trainers. 2020. Ethiopia.

Trendence, UK. 2017. *Teaching Excellence: The Student Perspective*. Research Commissioned by a Consortium of Students' Unions. London: Trendence.

UK Professional Standards Framework (UKPSF). 2011.

UK Standing Committee for Quality Assessment and Quality Assurance Agency. 2018. *The Revised UK Quality Code for Higher Education*. London.

UNESCO. 2015a. *The right to education and the teaching profession: Overview of the measures supporting the rights, status and working conditions of the teaching profession reported on by Member States*. Paris: UNESCO.

UNESCO. 2015b. *Teacher Policy Development Guide*. Paris: UNESCO.

UNESCO Bangkok Office. 2015. *Teachers in Asia Pacific: Status and Rights*. UNESCO. Paris and Bangkok Office.

UNESCO/ILO/UNICEF/UNDP/EI. 2018. *Joint Message from Ms Audrey Azoulay, Director-General of UNESCO, Guy Ryder, Director-General, International Labour Organization, Henrietta H. Fore, Executive Director, UNICEF, Achim Steiner, Administrator, UNDP and David Edwards, General Secretary, Education International (EI) on the occasion of World Teachers' Day: The right to education means the right to a qualified teacher*. 5 October.

UNESCO Institute of Statistics. 2016. *The world needs almost 69 million new teachers to reach the 2030 education goals.*

———. 2016. *Fact Sheet. No. 39.* UNESCO UIS.

United States Agency for International Development. 2011. *First principles: Designing effective pre-service teacher education programs.* American Institutes for Research.

Universities UK. 2017a. *Implementation of the Higher Education and Research Act 2017.*

_____. 2017b. *Review of the Teaching Excellence Framework–Year 2: Process, Results and Next Steps.*

_____. 2019. *The Future of the TEF: Report to the Independent Reviewer.* London: Universities UK.

F. Van As. 2018. *Communities of Practice as a Tool for Continuing Professional Development of Technology Teachers' Professional Knowledge.* International Journal of Technology and Design Education. 28(2): pp. 417–430.

N.D. Vaughan. 2010. *A Blended Community of Inquiry Approach: Linking Student Engagement and Course Redesign.* Internet and Higher Education. 13(1/2). pp. 60–65.

N. Vaughan and D.R. Garrison. 2006. *How Blended Learning Can Support a Faculty Development Community of Inquiry.* Journal of Asynchronous Learning Networks. 10(4). pp. 139–152.

Viet Nam Chamber of Commerce and Industry–United States Agency for International Development. 2019. *The Vietnam Provincial Competitiveness Index 2018.* Ha Noi.

E. Villegas-Reimers. 2003. *Teacher Professional Development: An International Review of the Literature.* UNESCO, International Institute for Educational Planning. Paris.

H. Williams. 2020. *Interview: The British Council Centres of Excellence in Teaching and Learning Project in Bangladesh.* Skype, 5 February.

World Bank and World Health Organization. 2011. *The World Report on Disability.*

World Bank. 2013. *Skilling up Vietnam: Preparing the workforce for a modern market economy – Vietnam Development Report 2014.* Washington, DC.

———. 2016. *Ukraine Economic Update.*

———. 2020a. *Bangladesh—Higher Education Quality Enhancement Project.* Accessed 8 March.

———. 2020B. *World Bank Country and Lending Groups.*

World Data Lab. 2019. *Papua New Guinea: Recovering but Still Off-Track.* Vienna.

Y. Zhao. 2010. Preparing globally competent teachers: A new imperative for teacher education. *Journal of Teacher Education.* 61(5). pp. 422–431.

Further Readings

PHILIPPINES

M. Curtis and J.P. Robinson. 2020. *Scaling Quality Education Calls for Scaling Effective Teacher Professional Development.* The Brookings Institution. 23 January. https://www.brookings.edu/blog/education-plus-development/2020/01/23/scaling-quality-education-calls-for-scaling-effective-teacher-professional-development/.

G. Oakley, R. King, and G. Scarparolo. 2018. *An Evaluation of ELLN Digital: Technology-Supported Teacher Professional Development on Early Language, Literacy and Numeracy for K-3 Teachers.* Quezon City: Foundation for Information Technology Education and Development. http://dl4d.org/wp-content/uploads/2019/03/ELLN-Digital-Evaluation.pdf.

UNITED KINGDOM

AdvanceHE. https://www.advance-he.ac.uk/.

Government of the United Kingdom. UK Government Collection on the Teaching Excellence and Student Outcomes Framework. https://www.gov.uk/government/collections/teaching-excellence-framework.

Office for Students. https://www.officeforstudents.org.uk/advice-and-guidance/teaching/.

Times Higher Education. https://www.timeshighereducation.com/policy/teaching-excellence-framework-tef.

WonkHE TEF commentary. https://wonkhe.com/tag/tef/.

VIET NAM

Programme Reform of TVET in Vietnam. 2019. 18 Teachers of LILAMA 2 International Technology College Ra Skill Level Equivalent to Skills Workers in Germany. https://www.tvet-vietnam.org/en/article/1605.18-teachers-of-lilama-2-international-technology-college-reached-a-skill-level-equivalent-to-a-skilled-worker-in-germany.html.

Programme Reform of TVET in Vietnam. 2018. Bosch Vietnam, the Directorate of Vocational Education and Training, LILAMA 2 International Technology College and GIZ Enter Into a Development Partnership to Prepare the Workforce for the Requirements of Industry 4.0 in Vietnam. https://www.tvet-vietnam.org/en/article/1502.bosch-vietnam-the-directorate-of-vocational-education-and-training-the-lilama-2-international-technology-college-and-giz-enter-into-a-development-partnership-to-prepare-the-workforce-for-the-requirements-of-industry-4-0-in-vietnam.html?sstr=Bosch.

GHANA

All key policy documents, resource materials, research reports, and external evaluation survey results can be
found on T-TEL's Learning Hub at http://www.t-tel.org/learning-hub.

UKRAINE

The Results Output Matrix is accessible at https://cutt.ly/vrYk7bH. Project reports are available at https://cutt.
ly/NrYkJ5V. Detailed descriptions of activities, terms of reference, reports, etc. are found at https://cutt.ly/
xrYkVDt. Also visit https://www.facebook.com/navchaemos.razom.

www.ingramcontent.com/pod-product-compliance
Lightning Source LLC
Chambersburg PA
CBHW050046220326
41599CB00045B/7297